Working lives in catering

By the same author

Freud and Society

Working lives in catering

Yiannis Gabriel

Routledge & Kegan Paul
London and New York

First published in 1988 by
Routledge & Kegan Paul Ltd
11 New Fetter Lane, London EC4P 4EE

Published in the USA by
Routledge & Kegan Paul Inc.
in association with Methuen Inc.
29 West 35th Street, New York, NY 10001

Set in Baskerville, 10 on 12 pt
by Input Typesetting Ltd, London SW19 8DR
and printed in Great Britain
by T. J. Press (Padstow) Ltd,
Padstow, Cornwall.

© Yiannis Gabriel 1988

No part of this book may be reproduced in
any form without permission from the publisher
except for the quotation of brief passages
in criticism

Library of Congress Cataloging in Publication Data

British Library CIP Data also available
ISBN 0–7102–0923–1

Contents

Preface	vii
Introduction	1
1 Home-cooking for thousands	18
2 The cooking factory	57
3 The fun food machine	93
4 Craft cooking for gentlemen	129
5 The small independent restaurant or café: The price of independence	142
6 Conclusions: Keeping the lid on	152
Appendix – the interview schedule	169
Notes	173
Bibliography and further reading	184
Index	188

Preface

Almost 10 per cent of British workers are currently employed in catering. This is a book based on the working lives of some 200 of these people.

I spent six months doing field research in kitchens, dining areas and catering offices, talking to people about their jobs and working conditions. Much of this time was spent observing cooks cooking, waiters waiting and managers managing. In addition, I carried out structured interviews with many of the management and staff in eight different catering establishments.

My primary concern was to express the feelings and views of these people in their own words, to describe their work and to document their relations with each other. Less significantly, I hoped to examine the nature of work in the rapidly expanding service sector and assess the impact of new technology and new management systems on its workforce.

What emerges from this study is a microcosm of workplace politics in contemporary Britain, an account of class relations at the point of production, and a portrait of a much-neglected but increasingly important sector of today's working class. Although the experiences of catering workers are in some ways unique, many of the industrial and economic realities which confront them are central to the study of the changing physiognomy of the working class in the 1980s.

Academic references and detailed social statistics in the text have been deliberately kept to a minimum; much of this information can be found in the lengthy notes to the Introduction.

This project resulted from discussions I had with Dr Tim Lang and it would have never materialized without his support; I am indebted to him. I also wish to thank several other friends who helped me with comments on earlier drafts and encouragement; my

Preface

special thanks to John Collee, David Robins and Jane Gabriel. David Mitchell, the Riverside House librarian at Thames Polytechnic, helped me gather statistical and other information on the catering industry from the jungle of existing sources, and I am indebted to him. Thanks are also due to some of my students at Thames Polytechnic who discussed their experiences in catering with me, to the staff of the Hollings Faculty at Manchester Polytechnic who gave me useful advice and to my colleagues in the Division of Organizational Studies at Thames Polytechnic who made it possible for me to carry out my field research during a six month research leave.

Above all I wish to thank the catering workers and managers who participated in my research. All of them generously gave me their time, ideas and support and I hope that this book does justice to their contribution. It is with regret that I must keep their identity as well as that of their employers confidential. Throughout this book, the names of people and places as well as small biographical details have been altered.

Introduction

Imagine yourself unemployed and looking for a job. You walk into your local Job Centre and are greeted by these cards, under the heading 'Latest Vacancies'. These jobs are advertised in a London Job Centre in March 1986. If you are young, unemployed and lack qualifications, if you are a married woman with children at school and badly need some cash

> Job: F/T and P/T Crew Members
> Wages: £2.10 at 18+, £1.60 at 16–17, meal, uniform
> Hours: Hours to suit – min 4 hrs per week
> Details: Bright cheerful staff 16–35 with clean appearance and confident outgoing personality to work for this world famous fast-food restaurant. Immediate start, good promotion prospects, hrs to suit. Will cook, clean and serve public. Training given. Must be articulate. No tattoos.
>
> ASK FOR JOB NUMBER 7703

> Job: Catering Assistant
> Wages: £91.90 p.w.
> Hours: F/T hours T.B.A.
> Details: Age 18+ hygiene-conscious person reqd for local hospital to assist in kitchen in basic preparation of meals and to assist in serving food over counter and to maintain cleaning of serving areas. Exp preferred. Common sense and refs essential. Application form pro.
>
> ASK FOR JOB 3908

1

Introduction

Job: Kitchen Porter
Wages: £80.62 p.w.
Hours: 11–7 pm Mon–Fri
Details: Age 18–40 kitchen porter needed for catering company. Duties include washing plates, floors, heavy duty cleaning. Experience not necessary. Refs reqd.

ASK FOR JOB NUMBER 1119

Job: Assistant Cook
Wages: £93 p/w
Hours: Mon–Fri 7–3.30 pm
Details: Experienced cook reqd for an industrial canteen. Will be preparing breakfasts, lunches, etc. Must have at least five years experience preferably industrial. C & G 706/1 or 2 an advantage.

ASK FOR JOB NUMBER 3818

---

to make ends meet, if you are a middle-aged man laid off for a couple of years and beginning to despair of ever finding another job, then your eyes will stop at these advertisements.

At the time of writing, catering is one of the few industries which can still offer jobs. It is often the only door open to people whose age, education, language, and lack of qualifications rule them out for everything else. But how much is known about working in catering? What is the reality behind the job descriptions?

Catering is a large and constantly expanding industry,[1] providing a wide range of products and services. The three-course meal eaten by candlelight on a white tablecloth is as much part of it as the portion of fish and chips consumed on the street corner, the sandwich eaten during a break at work or the traditional stodgy mass served on hospital plates.

This diversity of products and services is mirrored in the great variety of the workforce. Catering workers come from every segment of the working class, skilled as well as unskilled, female and male, full-time and part-time, seasonal and permanent, young and old. Some work in large organizations employing hundreds of people, some in small restaurants employing only a few individuals and some work for themselves. Many catering workers come from ethnic minorities and immigrant groups or from the vast pool of young workers, all of whom have been consistently neglected by social research.

In fact, catering workers frequently complain that they are taken for granted. They are rarely presented in the mass media; politicians and academic researchers who often talk about the 'service sector' rarely trouble themselves to find out what catering work is like. Even the public with whom catering workers come into daily contact seldom seems to register their existence. Sharon, an 18-year-old student hoping to go to medical school, works weekends in a fast-food store in the West End:

> You serve hundreds of people here each day. Some of them are regular, I see them every Saturday. But most of them hardly seem to notice you – all they want is to get served as soon as possible and that's all that matters. Sometimes I think that this uniform makes me invisible.

Mary Price, in her late fifties, cooks in a modern frozen-food kitchen:

> Working in catering you feel sometimes that your job lacks dignity. Kitchen ladies and catering staff in general are treated as inferior people by everyone.

The low status of catering work is well-documented. Most catering jobs are low-paid with poor job security and union representation and with high concentrations of part-time employees and women workers. Catering wages are consistently low – waitresses are at the bottom of the female wage league; only hairdressers earn less. Kitchen porters and bar staff are at the bottom of the male league (only agricultural workers earn less) with chefs and cooks only slightly higher.[2] Catering managers are by a considerable distance at the bottom of managerial earnings.

These conditions partly account for the low prestige of most catering work. But the real stigma may have deeper origins. Catering work is service work and catering workers have suffered as a result of the historical connotations of service as servitude. Manufacturing workers sell their labour to their employers but are answerable to no one else. Service workers also sell their labour to their employers, but do so under the scrutiny of the customer who is paying to be served, obeyed and entertained. This gives catering

Introduction

workers a sense of subservience which is not associated with other jobs. Manufacturing workers work in places which are designated as workplaces during hours which are designated as work hours. By contrast, the waiter's workplace is the customer's place of enjoyment and relaxation; the cook's time on the job is the customer's time off. The sense of servitude which results is heightened by the requirement that catering workers must be discreet to the point of invisibility. This predicament has not changed with the transition from domestic to industrial service.

This book seeks to make more visible what has been largely invisible by giving voice to those who spend their working lives in catering – the cook who prepares the food, the porter who brings the meals to hospital wards, the dinner woman who serves our children at school, the young man or woman who serves us in the fast food outlet, the washer-upper, the supervisor and the manager. These workers, far from being an untypical minority on the margins of the working class, are now part of the majority working in the service industries.

The McDonaldization of the economy?

It has become commonplace to argue that advanced industrial societies are rapidly becoming service societies. As employment in the manufacturing sector declines, an ever-increasing proportion of the workforce is employed in the tertiary or service sector. This includes finance and insurance, education, health, transportation, retailing, communication and mass media, repairing and servicing, cleaning, catering, entertainment and tourism.

Between 1971 and 1984 manufacturing and construction in the United Kingdom lost 2.5 million jobs, while the service sector increased by nearly 2 million; the service industries now account for 62 per cent of all jobs as against 52 per cent in 1971 and 46 per cent in 1961. Similar trends have occurred in other industrialized countries. In the United States, for example, 14.7 million more people worked in the service sector in 1984 than in 1975; remarkably, the new catering jobs created during this period outnumber *total* employment in the motor and steel industries. With employment in the manufacturing sector having shrunk to only 25 per cent of the workforce and agriculture accounting for another 3 per cent, employment in the service sector has reached a massive 72 per cent.[3]

As employment in the manufacturing industries has continued to decline, hopes for the creation of new jobs and future prosperity have been largely pinned on the continuing expansion of the service economy. It is now regarded as axiomatic that 'employment in the services is a critical issue for industrial countries' (Gershuny and Miles, 1983:1). Some, like Daniel Bell, have argued that the increasing demand for services is closely linked to the higher standards of living and the growth of new and higher human needs – for health, information, education and leisure.[4] Bell regards the shift from manufacturing to services as the key to a massive economic and social transformation on the same scale as the shift from agriculture to manufacture. For him and the enthusiasts of the service economy, the coming of the post-industrial society will redeem humanity from the worst consequences of the industrial revolution. As the smokestack industries are replaced by new high-tech establishments, physical labour is replaced by mental labour, leading to an upgrading of people's skills and better working conditions.

But not every one has been so optimistic about the prospects offered by the new service sector. In spite of the growth of business and professional services, many of the jobs in this sector are low-paid, unskilled and non-unionised. Interestingly, most of them are 'women's jobs'.[5] This is immediately apparent from the list of the ten most secure jobs according to the US Department of Labor Statistics:

- secretaries
- nursing auxiliaries
- cleaners
- retail assistants
- cashiers
- nurses
- lorry drivers
- fast-food workers
- clerks
- waiters and waitresses[6]

But, critics of the 'service economy' are not only sceptical about the quality of the jobs in the service sector; more importantly, they question the continuing prosperity of the service sector if a nation's manufacturing base is allowed to erode. Lee Iacocca, the flam-

Introduction

boyant chairman of Chrysler Corporation and one of America's most highly regarded executives, has responded to the 'McDonaldization of the economy' with the comment that 'we can't afford to become a nation of video arcades, drive-in banks, and McDonald's hamburger stands.' Jonathan Gershuny has likewise suggested that a firm manufacturing base is indispensable for the continuing success of the service sector. Many of the service workers, he argues, are either indirectly involved in the manufacture of goods (engineers, draughtsmen, etc.) or are serving manufacturing industry (office workers, cleaners, business consultants, etc.); after careful examination of statistical data, Gershuny estimates that less than a quarter of those in the service sector are actually engaged in the provision of services, while the rest are directly or indirectly servicing the manufacturing sector (1978:113).

It is evident that there is no general agreement on even what constitutes the service sector.[7] What there is agreement on is that, in spite of its importance, there is great scarcity of field research on the service sector, when compared with the wealth of material drawn from manufacturing.[8] In addition, official statistics and economic indicators like the FT Index and the Dow Jones Industrial Average are heavily biased towards manufacturing, making it difficult to obtain reliable information about what is perhaps the most vital sector of the economy. In this respect, the situation has not changed much since 1968 when Fuchs described the service sector of the economy as the neglected 'stepchild of economic research'.

I hope that this book will make a contribution to the discussion of some of the key issues in this area:

- Is the increase in service employment due to the intrinsically low productivity of labour in this sector?
- Are services as prone to replacement of labour by capital as manufacturing?
- What kinds of jobs are available in the service industries and what are the likely effects of new technology on these jobs?
- What are the relations between managers and workers in the new service industries and how do they differ from workplace politics in the manufacturing industries?
- What is the future of trade unions and worker militance following the decline of their traditional industrial strongholds?

The changing face of catering

If employment in the service sector has emerged as a critical issue for the future of industrial societies, catering is emerging as a critical industry in this sector. In the past twenty or thirty years, our eating and drinking habits have changed more than we could ever have imagined. It is not just what we eat that has changed, but also where we eat and how we eat. Take-away meals, fast food, health food, ethnic restaurants and cafés, wine bars and haute-cuisine restaurants are all central features of what has been described as a revolution in eating habits and tastes.

During this period, the character of the catering industry itself has been undergoing a profound transformation. Traditional catering was in essence a 'people's industry', depending for its success on the social and technical skills of its personnel, their ingenuity and hard work, their commitment and 'attitude'. The nature and the quality of service as well as the satisfaction and loyalty of the clients depended crucially on the human factor.[9]

Some management theorists have argued that reliance on the human factor accounts for the backwardness of traditional catering and the service industries in general. Professor Theodore Levitt and his colleagues at the Harvard Business School, for example, have criticized management in the service sector for seeking higher productivity and a better service not in the planning and control of the work task but 'in the *performer* of the task. This is the paralysing legacy of our inherited attitudes: the solution to improved service is viewed as being dependent on the performers of that service' (1972:43). By contrast, argues Levitt, the rise of productivity in the manufacturing industries throughout the twentieth century has resulted from a systematic planning of the work process and the effective application of technology to minimize reliance on the discretion of the performer of the task.[10] Control is not exercised by arbitrary supervisors exhorting greater effort from the workers, but becomes incorporated in the process itself, the moving assembly line, the standardized work practices, the machines and the products themselves.

Levitt recommends the same strategy to managements in the service industries as the recipe for improved service and efficiency. He refers to it as the *industrialization of service* (Levitt, 1981:41). Modern catering seems to be responding to such calls. In contrast to traditional catering, it impresses with the range and complexity of its technical hardware, the meticulous planning, standardization and marketing of its products and services, the fragmentation of its production techniques. Reliance on the human factor, the cook's artistry, the waiter's manners, the manager's conviviality or the washer-upper's hard work are gradually being replaced by planning and technology.[11] The success of the organization no longer relies on people performing their tasks better but rather on a better organization of tasks, indeed on an organization of tasks such as makes the distinction between good and poor performance redundant.

If the fast-food industry is regarded as the pioneering vanguard of catering, then it can be argued with justification that the industry is changing from a people's industry to a high-tech industry, modelling itself on the more successful sectors of manufacturing. Instead of striving for a high-cost, personal service, modern catering proposes a low-cost, standardized but reliable one. Professor Levitt's description of the fast-food outlet is an apt outline of this trend:

> It is a machine that produces, with the help of totally unskilled machine tenders, a highly polished product. Through painstaking attention to total design and facilities planning, everything is built integrally into the machine itself, into the technology of the system. The only choice available to the attendant is to operate it exactly as the designers intended. (1972:46)

Much of catering is still run along traditional lines; but rationalizing trends are evident everywhere. Sophisticated technology, standardized products, fragmented and routinized production, careful planning are dramatically changing the appearance of eating and drinking places. Frozen food, processed in food factories which at times resemble assembly lines and at times petro-chemical refineries, finds its way not only on fast-food trays, but also in school dining-rooms and hospital wards as well as in haute-cuisine restaurants. Even the jargon begins to sound like that of industrial production – cooks are re-classified as 'material handlers', waiters as 'interface workers', others as crew-members or thawers-outers.

Technology and control at work

- What are the implications of these changes on the work and working conditions of people working in catering?
- Does the new emphasis on planning bring order and comfort in place of the chaos and heat of traditional kitchens?
- Does new catering technology liberate workers from the drudgery of boring, repetitive and arduous work, allowing them to exercise their skills and intelligence?
- Or, does new catering technology exacerbate feelings of powerlessness and meaninglessness, by turning them into ever less significant cogs of vast production machines?[12]

Our personal experience with home catering technology may justify a rather optimistic attitude; a dish-washer reduces the tedium of washing up, a food processor replaces energy- and time-consuming whisks, shredders, mixers and graters, a deep freezer and micro-wave oven permit better and more economical planning. As has long been recognized, however, technology at the place of work is not 'just machines'; it also involves knowhow, methods, recipes, and 'ways of doing things', in short, technological systems. In arguing that catering is becoming a 'high-tech' industry we are not merely drawing attention to the sophisticated hardware which is advertised in the trade magazines and annually exhibited in catering exhibitions but also to the software, the ways in which the service is planned, controlled and executed.

This aspect of the service economy has never been fully explored. There exists, however, an abundance of research material drawn from the manufacturing sector, which forms part of a lively debate on the 'labour process'. This debate was sparked off by the publication in 1974 of Harry Braverman's book *Labor and Monopoly Capital*, one of the most frequently quoted works in the social sciences. Braverman's main thesis (summed up in the subtitle of his book 'The Degradation of Work in the Twentieth Century') is that throughout the twentieth century, the working classes of Europe and America have been progressively deskilled thus losing control of production. In contrast to craft production which afforded a substantial degree of autonomy and control to the skilled artisan, mass production concentrates control in the hands of management, while the workers 'sink to the level of general and undifferentiated labor power, adaptable to a large range of simple tasks' (1974:121).

Introduction

The chief agent through which this degradation of work has been accomplished is, in the view of Braverman, *Scientific Management*, the school of management thought whose principles were first articulated at the turn of the century by F. W. Taylor. Taylor argued that management should claim the initiative in production by organizing the work process according to scientific principles instead of relying on the workers' traditional skills, abilities and willingness to work hard.

The underpinning principle of Taylorism, in Braverman's view, is the separation of *conception* from *execution*, whereby the managers assume 'the burden of gathering together all of the traditional knowledge which in the past has been possessed by the workmen and then of classifying, tabulating, and reducing this knowledge to rules, laws and formulae' (Taylor, 1967:36). Production should be broken down to numerous simple tasks and the execution of each task should be standardized, after careful study, according to the one best way of doing it. Workers should then be hired capable and willing to carry out these tasks according to strictly laid-down guidelines in return for purely financial incentives. The huge increases in productivity resulting from the application of his principles, argued Taylor, would permit far greater remuneration for the workers and greater still profits for capital. By replacing management's arbitrary powers with scientifically determined standards of work, Taylor felt that scientific management opened the path for co-operation between management and workers.

Social scientists have delighted in criticizing Taylor's belief that he had laid the foundations for industrial harmony, his near caricature of the worker as an 'economic man' concerned solely with maximizing his/her pay packet and his entirely mechanistic conception of production. In Braverman's view, however, his principles of separation of conception from execution, fragmentation, standardization and routinization have, throughout the twentieth century, been instrumental in 'shaping the modern corporation and all institutions of capitalist society which carry on labor processes' (1974:86) and achieve their consummation in Henry Ford's assembly lines. Braverman saw Taylorism as the unfolding of the inner logic of capitalism, leading to the gradual impoverishment, degradation and reduction of the worker and bolstering capital's control over the production process. A deskilled working class is an emasculated working class, reduced to a mere factor of production, unable to exercise its power at the one place where its power lies, the workplace.

A pioneering feature of Braverman's analysis is the extension of his argument to the service sector, observing Taylorism in offices, restaurants and retail outlets. Addressing explicitly the catering industry, he notes that new frozen food technologies are destroying the 'ancient and valuable craft' of cooking, even in its 'last stronghold, luxury and gourmet cooking' and concludes:

> As in so many other fields of work, the simplification and rationalization of skills in the end destroy these skills, and, with the skills becoming ever more scarce, the new processes become ever more inevitable – because of the shortage of skilled labor! (1974:370)

This is the point where Braverman's pessimistic assessment converges with Levitt's enthusiastic description of the fast-food outlet as a machine operated by 'totally unskilled machine tenders'. In their view, catering and the service sector industries are likely to follow the path laid by the manufacturing sector. Deskilling, mechanization and standardization are seen by both as the inevitable response of modern catering to the call for greater control, productivity and efficiency. This trend, however, cannot be regarded as unproblematic without substantial field research into different areas of catering.

Nor can Braverman's theory be accepted without qualifications. In spite of the considerable (and at times uncritical) acclaim with which it has been received, several weaknesses have been pointed out. From the right, it has been pointed out that new technologies and new methods of production may dissolve ancient skills but they also give rise to new ones, often superior to the old ones; instead of deskilling, personnel theorists and practitioners prefer to talk of 'reskilling', arguing that under the right conditions workers welcome technological change, and experience greater control and autonomy in their work. Braverman has generally been criticized for clinging to an idealized notion of the traditional artisan, for identifying technology with Taylorism and losing sight of the progressive and liberating potential of technology.

From the left, Braverman has been criticized for disregarding worker resistance to Taylorism, for adhering to a rather mechanistic conception of skill and, more generally, for over-emphasizing the importance of Taylorism in strengthening capitalist control over production at the expense of other factors. Braverman has also been criticized for abstracting the workplace from the rest of society and under-estimating the effects on the labour process of institutions such as the family, the educational system, the media and especially the state on what goes on inside.[13]

At the heart of many responses to Braverman's thesis has been a challenge to his concept of control, and a considerable research effort, both theoretical and empirical, has been devoted to an elaboration and refinement of this concept. Unfortunately, very little of this effort has focused on the service industries which form such an important part of Braverman's argument. Catering, with its recent espousal of sophisticated technology and modern management techniques, is a fertile terrain for pursuing the issues raised by this debate.

The field research

In planning the research I decided to study a small number of establishments ranging from traditional to modern catering. In addition, I decided that half of these establishments should be large, bureaucratic organizations and the rest small-scale ones. After preliminary discussions, I got access to the following catering places:

- a traditional mass catering unit in a hospital
- a modern frozen-food unit in a community centre
- three outlets of a fast-food chain
- a traditional fish-and-chips restaurant
- a kebab house
- a gentlemen's club

Early in the research I also had plans to investigate an haute-cuisine restaurant. It soon became clear, however, that a search for a 'representative' restaurant of this type was futile; after preliminary discussions in a few places I realized that they were so different from each other that there was no real justification for concentrating on any one of them and the idea was dropped; undoubtedly this sector of catering deserves a study all to itself. It is also true that the limited existing literature on catering has focused precisely on such establishments.[14]

Field research was new to me and I approached it with considerable apprehension. Contrary to workers and managers in the automobile industry, catering staff are not used to social researchers taking an interest in their working lives. Many of the older workers could simply see no point to my study until I explained that I was hoping to write a book describing their experiences and outlooks. 'But what do you find in catering, love?' some of the older workers would ask, and I would explain the reasons why I chose catering as my area of study – the industry's size, its ability to generate jobs for young people, the fact that everybody has some experience of having a meal outside the home, but few appreciate what goes on behind the counter or in the kitchen.

In the larger establishments, word of my research would rapidly spread among the catering staff and the majority of the people would approach me with a mixture of curiosity, interest and scepticism. Younger workers, on the whole, found it easier to understand the reasons of my research than older ones. A few were suspicious about my motives. One group of dining-room assistants in a mood of general hilarity admitted to me after a few days 'We thought, you know, that you were a spy when you first came here,' only for one of them to reassure me, 'Don't listen to them, love, they are only pulling your leg. They were all queueing up to talk to you.'

I found that being an immigrant to the United Kingdom myself was a considerable advantage; in the first place, it partly accounted for what many people saw as my eccentric fascination with their working lives. More importantly, it placed me outside the class structure of British society and minimized suspicions that I might have been interested in 'spying for the other side' or 'for headquarters'. As people gradually came to understand the reasons for my research, many of their natural inhibitions seemed to vanish and they treated me with great generosity, answering my questions and helping me in many ways to organize the project. I was often struck by people's willingness to answer my questions at the end of a long working day or in their free time.

During my entire project I only encountered one refusal and two reluctant interviewees. The vast majority of people, once they had understood the aim and object of my research, gave me full support and assistance. 'Go on, young man,' they would say, 'write your book and tell them what it's like to work in this place.' For many, my presence was a welcome break from the routine, and for a few it was an opportunity to talk about things which they could not discuss with their workmates. 'Now what are *you* going to do about

Introduction

all this?' I was asked once by a foreign catering assistant, after she had recounted a lifetime of oppression and suffering.

In each of the larger establishments, I spent the first few days informally explaining to people what I was hoping to do. During this period I tried to talk to most managers and union officials, covering a specific number of points but not following a fixed schedule of questions. After a few days, I started using a structured interview schedule. I endeavoured to interview as many people as possible. In particular, I tried to ensure that no class of employees would be missed. In catering, where some of the staff work only night-shifts or part-time on weekends, and where substantial numbers of staff are not fluent in English, it is easy to obtain a partial picture by interviewing only those individuals who happen to be there during the researcher's visits. I tried to interview three or four individuals each day, but there were occasions when everybody was so busy that interviewing anyone was out of the question. The rest of the time was spent observing working methods and work relations and having informal chats with people while they went about their business. I kept copious notes of these conversations and was often teased; 'Dear me, what I wouldn't give to know what goes in those blue books of yours,' I was frequently told with a wink, and on occasion: 'Just make sure you don't leave those blue books with all that's in them lying around. I wouldn't like them to know what I'm telling you.'

In the hospital and community-centre catering organizations I interviewed more than three-quarters of the staff, while in the three fast-food outlets covered I interviewed about one-quarter of the workforce. The gentlemen's club had only seven members of staff and I interviewed all of them. These interviews took place in private sessions lasting about an hour. By contrast, the owners of the fish and chips restaurant and of the kebab house chose to be interviewed in the presence of others who were, as it happened, members of their family.

The schedule of questions was developed during the preliminary stage of the research. No proper pilot study was possible within the time available, so some modifications had to be made after the first six interviews, as it became clear that some important areas had not been adequately covered and some of the original questions were ambiguous. For instance, the question 'How safe is your job?' was taken by some people to refer to physical safety and by others to security of employment, so it had to be re-phrased.

The interviews contained in all about ninety questions (reproduced in the Appendix), of which about thirty were open-ended. They covered personal employment history, attitudes towards the job, technology, the employer and work in general, relations with other workers and management, attitudes towards unions and industrial relations, views on the catering industry as a whole and personal cooking and eating habits. The respondents' answers were recorded in writing. This created some problems in recording verbatim quotes, but as my respondents could see what I was writing they could check for accuracy. In addition, the time it took me to record their answers gave them the opportunity to develop their thoughts, explain and qualify their responses.

While the overall approach was uniform, a certain amount of flexibility was necessary in the phrasing as well as the sequence of questions. A special effort was made not to try to pigeon-hole responses. Ambivalence, incompleteness and inconsistencies in people's attitudes and conceptions were accepted and acknowledged, as was also the volatility of responses. On several occasions, individuals changed their mind with respect to a particular question where some people first described their job as 'fairly good' and then towards the end of the interview as 'not too good'.

One of the researcher's perennial problems is the split between his/her desire for crisp, precise answers, which can be easily coded and classified, and the need to do justice to the infinite range and complexities of human experience. Cultural background and age seemed to have a great influence on people's answers to interview questions; British and younger respondents were much more likely to answer in concise, unqualified and unambiguous ways. By contrast, some of the foreign and older respondents gave me qualified answers even to the most straightforward questions and were much more willing to accept ambivalence in their feelings. For instance, a West Indian hospital kitchen porter answered virtually every one of my questions with 'It depends, sometimes . . .', while an Italian assistant head cook at the same place told me in the course of one interview both that she loved that hospital and that she could not last out at her job for five more minutes. It is not easy to know the extent to which these differences in the ways people respond to interview questions reflect genuine differences in their experiences and the extent to which they reflect different norms of expression and communication.

Introduction

Places visited

Each chapter of this book focuses on one type of catering establishment. Chapter 1 examines the catering department of a large and historic hospital in central London, referred to in this study as Saint Theresa's. A staff of nearly 100, including some 20 qualified cooks, prepared over 2,500 meals per day for patients as well as for medical and other staff; they used very traditional mass catering methods and rather old-fashioned equipment. In many respects, this operation could be described as 'home-cooking writ large', relying on the abilities and skills of the staff to provide a satisfactory service. Protected for a long time from the direct ravages of the market, this catering unit had recently come under threat of government cutbacks and potential competition from external contractors, resulting in a forceful management drive to reduce costs. New work practices, new rosters and some new equipment had been introduced two years before my visit, against strong opposition from the union. Painful memories of the confrontation were still fresh in people's minds. The workforce included many older foreign workers as well as an increasing number of younger staff, many of whom had or were getting catering qualifications.

Chapter 2 deals with the second organization I investigated, the catering network of an urban community centre in North England, referred to here as Michael Lansby. The centre includes a comprehensive school, a college of further education, an adult education college, and a public library as well as a whole host of educational and recreational facilities. A kitchen staffed by about 20 women (most of them unqualified) produced more than 2,500 meals per day which were frozen and stored. These meals were then distributed to the satellite dining-areas as well as to six local schools, where they were defrosted and served. This catering department had been planned twelve years earlier, employed modern cooking and freezing equipment and was regarded as a showpiece for sophisticated catering hardware. The eating places varied from traditional cafeterias to dining-areas modelled on fast-food outlets. The department employed nearly eighty staff (managerial, cooking and waitressing), of whom a large number of whom were women working part-time.

The next three establishments I visited, described in Chapter 3, were London stores of one of the leading hamburger chains, Fun Food here. Each carried out between 700 and 10,000 counter transactions per day and employed between 40 and 90 staff, many of whom were part-time and wholly unqualified in catering. The product, the restaurant lay-out, the production and serving methods, were all carefully planned and standardized. Sophisticated cooking equipment was used to re-process uniform raw materials. Staff, all of them under 25 years old, had virtually no discretion on any matters and their work amounted to little more than the execution of simple routines.

The last three establishments in my study were much smaller-scale operations. Chapter 4 describes a gentlemen's club in the Midlands which employed rather antiquated equipment to provide a high-quality menu with a choice of two main dishes. Between 12 and 30 meals were prepared and served by a staff of 7 women, 6 of whom had more than five years of service. The last two establishments, covered in Chapter 5, were a fish and chips restaurant and a kebab house both in east London; these were small-scale entrepreneurial concerns run primarily by their owners, along with the owners' families and a few part-time and casual staff. The success of both of these restaurants depended on individual ingenuity, informal work arrangements and sheer hard work rather than on the use of sophisticated labour-saving machinery.

These eight establishments do not by any means cover the gamut of catering organizations, but they do cover a broad spectrum; both large and small establishments were investigated, private and public organizations, technologically advanced and relatively primitive, individual as well as mass catering. In addition, almost every type of catering worker is represented in the study.[15] Apart from a personal fascination with cooking, it was the diversity as well as the similarities of the working lives of these people which made my excursions into the catering industry so rewarding.[16]

CHAPTER 1
Home-cooking for thousands

It's a job, it's the money I want. I don't come here for no friends, I don't come here for no England. I come here for one thing, to better myself, do my job, get more money; then I go back to Jamaica, there is no place like home. I don't want to be an old man in this cold, hard country. I run my own life, no one else. I prefer to keep out of people's way, I mind my own business.

Mr John Grant, 53,
kitchen-porter at Saint Theresa's

Saint Theresa's hospital is a large and historic teaching hospital in the heart of London. Its 36 wards and 800 patients' beds are scattered in several different buildings, some of which are several hundred years old. The catering department of the hospital, providing daily around 2,500 meals, was selected for the purposes of this project as representative of traditional mass catering. It also provides an example of catering in the National Health Service, a truly massive operation accounting for about 6 per cent of the budget, serving 1.5 million meals per day and involving the equivalent of 30,000 full-time workers.[1]

The catering department at Saint Theresa's evolved over the years as the hospital's needs and its resources changed. Cooking methods have changed little since the 1960s, relying on the ability, judgment and skill of the staff to prepare a highly varied product, in accordance with traditional methods. Catering technology is relatively simple and much of the equipment is dated. This does not mean that there have been no changes in recent years. In fact, no other organization which I visited had experienced quite the same extent of changes as Saint Theresa's.

Home-cooking for thousands

In the early 1960s, catering staff at Saint Theresa's were almost entirely foreign; Italian, Greek, Polish, Czech and Spanish workers and indeed whole 'families' were employed in jobs which were generally scorned by the indigenous workforce. At the time, there were no qualified staff. The conditions of service were poor and the wage level well below what most British people would work for. Miss Summerfield, the catering manager, had started work as a junior manager in 1962:

> In those days it was difficult to attract British people here, given our location, the low wages and few possibilities. It was impossible to employ qualified cooks and we employed mostly people from the continent. For them it was the only work they could get; for us they were the only people we could get. We frequently employed whole families, husbands and wives, nephews and nieces.

At the time, the department employed 180 people, working in two main kitchens and serving two separate dining-rooms, several snack-bars as well as separate dining-rooms for non-resident staff, consultants, registrars, senior nurses and other nursing staff. Over the years the operation was rationalized, with the elaborate hierarchic divisions of the hospital gradually ironed out, at least as far as catering was concerned. At present, there is one kitchen, located on the fourth floor of a main building, where food is prepared for the patients as well as for serving in the two main, adjoining dining-rooms. They are located in the basement of the building and only one of them is open for 24 hours a day. Nurses and physicians still have a separate dining area each but are served the same meals as are served in the main dining-rooms.

The majority of the main meals are prepared in the kitchen and then transferred in trolleys to the dining-rooms in the basement and to the wards. A four-weekly menu of three main courses for lunch and for supper provides the basis for each day's cooking assignments. In addition the department has a special diets' kitchen where some 100 meals are prepared daily for diabetics or patients with special nutritional requirements.

In the last few years, the kitchen staff have been able to cater for an increasing number of 'special functions', preparing high-quality meals for between 16 and 200 guests. Up to 100 such functions are catered for annually. This has been possible because of a drastic change in the profile of the workforce. As more and more qualified catering staff have turned to the National Health Service for employment in recent years, the number of qualified cooks and chefs at Saint Theresa's rose from 3 to about 20. Most of them were in their teens or early twenties and came fresh from catering college.

At the time of my visit, the catering department employed 'on paper' 103 staff, but in practice only some 88, including 5 management, 3 office workers, 38 kitchen staff, 10 trolley-porters and 28 dining-room staff. About half of them had up to 10 years of service and twenty of them, nearly all foreign, had more than 15 years of service. In all the department employed 28 foreign or immigrant staff, all but a couple of whom had worked there for more than ten years.

The department was run by Miss Summerfield and three young assistant catering managers, one in charge of the kitchen, one in charge of the dining areas and one responsible for the store-rooms and for the office. In addition, Mr Gorman, the district catering manager, was based in the hospital and was mostly involved in long-term planning as well as in catering for special functions.

'The changes'

At the time of my visit, the catering department had emerged from a traumatic period of two or three years during which management had implemented a programme of reorganization and rationalization, what people in the department called 'the changes'. These changes were aimed at countering cheerful chaos, brought about during the years when 'the trustees automatically picked up the bill'. These years were over and, in view of the government's threats of privatization, management took the opportunity to impose a new rigorous system of work. The changes involved 'flexible work arrangements' with mobility of staff from section to section, new job descriptions which did away with traditional lines of demarcation and, most importantly, a new rostering system which dramatically reduced the amount of overtime clocked by staff.

In addition, in place of kitchen and dining-room superintendents new assistant managers had been appointed to run these sections, replacing a laissez-faire tradition and lax discipline with tighter managerial control. Overtime had been generously clocked previously and petty pilfering was rampant, especially at weekends when no managers were present. 'Everyone was on the fiddle in those days,' I was told by Vassilis Pappas, a porter of many years' service, who added, 'but then, with the wages and the conditions we had how else could we survive?' Under the new stricter regime, a manager was always present at weekends. Staff no longer received free meals and food returned from the wards and dining-rooms had to be thrown away in the presence of a supervisor.

These changes took place after considerable struggle. Management were aware that they had to 'take the union on' in order to implement their plan, but approached it as a challenge. The union, NUPE, was unwilling to talk about the changes which were then unilaterally implemented. The result was a general ban on overtime and a strike by portering staff. After severe divisions emerged in its ranks, the union side was forced to accept the changes, leaving many staff embittered and disillusioned.

The majority of the older, foreign cooks and porters left Saint Theresa's. As a way of implementing their plan, management had relied on an active recruiting policy. Cooks were recruited directly from catering colleges, while for the other positions people *without* catering experience were preferred. Mr Sprake, one of the managers, explained the aims of their recruitment policy:

> We interview short-listed people thoroughly. We are very selective; we want people who accept the rules and regulations, we want reliable people, people with whom we don't have to bargain all the time. Cooks are recruited mostly from outside London and are attracted by the prospect of free accommodation [which is provided]. We have to be careful ... we don't want people who want a good time in London. Porters are recruited locally – they are 25 to 55 years old, with family responsibilities. Many of them have been made redundant in their previous jobs. We prefer people from outside catering, who haven't picked up bad habits elsewhere.[2]

The union membership in the catering department had been drastically altered as a result of 'the changes'; in the kitchen, where the union had had 100 per cent membership, it lost nearly half its members, and most of the younger, qualified cooks chose not to join. Among the dining staff, however, union membership since 'the changes' rose from less than half to virtually everyone. Mike Robins, the Branch Secretary of NUPE, said:

> The trauma of the last two or three years left us in disarray.

> We succumbed during 'the changes' and we lost many of our members, some left the hospital, some left the union. Build-up of solidarity since then has been slow, . . . downstairs rather than upstairs.

Deep scars and divisions were still in evidence during my visit at Saint Theresa's. Many of my discussions with workers and managers returned to 'the changes', which had had a profound impact on them. Many of their attitudes and feelings were shaped by their experiences throughout that traumatic period or, in the case of those workers who had been recruited subsequently, by what they had heard and what they had believed about these events. There was almost a mythological quality about these events – everyone recognized their importance but there was no agreement about what had happened.

The field research

The sheer variety of people employed at Saint Theresa's, with their different views and perspectives and the great complexity of the catering operation, made it an ideal place to study mass catering. I spent five weeks at Saint Theresa's, observing the way the department was run, having informal conversations with nearly all the staff and I carried out 59 structured interviews. These 59 individuals were not a random sample of Saint Theresa's staff, several of whom could not be contacted due to sickness or holiday leave, but a stratified one; I endeavoured to include in my sample the same

TABLE 1.1
Distribution of sample at Saint Theresa's by type of work

Position	Number in department	Number in sample
Management and office	8	6
Cooks (all ranks)	22	19 (6)
Kitchen-porters	16	10 (4)
Trolley-porters	14	7 (3)
Dining staff	28	17 (7)
TOTAL	88 (28)	59 (20)

Note: Figures in parentheses are the number of foreign workers in each group. The storeman has been included with the kitchen-porters and the charge-hand with the trolley-porters.

ratios of foreign staff and women as in the department as a whole. I also made sure that the percentage of staff in my sample living in hospital accommodation was the same as that of the department as a whole. Finally, I tried to ensure that the length of service in my sample matched its distribution in the group as a whole.

Twenty of the 28 foreign workers at Saint Theresa's were included in the sample, 33 of the 44 women and 15 of the 20 staff living in hospital accommodation. The average length of service in the sample was 9 years. Table 1.2 reveals the long-term change in the profile of the workforce.

TABLE 1.2
Length of service of sample at Saint Theresa's

	M	C	KP	TP	D	All
Less than 2 years	3	11	2	3	3	22
2–5 years	3	1	5 (1)	0	2 (1)	11 (2)
5–15 years	0	4 (3)	2 (2)	1	2 (1)	9 (6)
More than 15 years	0	3 (3)	1 (1)	3 (3)	10 (5)	17 (12)
TOTAL	6	19 (6)	10 (4)	7 (3)	17 (7)	59 (20)

Notes: Figures in parentheses are those of foreign workers. In this and all the tables which follow, the following shorthand has been adopted:

M : Management and office staff
C : Cooks (all grades)
KP : Kitchen-porters
TP : Trolley-porters
D : Dining-room staff including supervisors

These figures give a clear indication of the two different types of staff employed at Saint Theresa's, the older, untrained, foreign workers recruited in the 1950s and 1960s and the younger, largely trained and British workers recruited in the past 5 years. What the figures cannot quite portray is the large heterogeneity of this group of workers; the catering department of Saint Theresa's was like a vast collage of human histories, a place where different cultures, ideas and languages met and mixed. Young women having recently arrived from Wales and living on hospital accommodation worked side by side with middle-aged West Indian women supporting large families, Spanish, Italian and Portuguese women with grown-up children, being supervised by Irish women approaching retirement. Teenaged cooks straight from catering college worked together with

Cypriot and Algerian cooks, being served by Scottish, Spanish or West Indian kitchen-porters.

Most of the people to whom I talked had many stories to relate to me, incidents that marked their histories at Saint Theresa's. It would be an injustice to them if I presented their views merely as aggregate statistics. Statistics frequently conceal deep personal experiences. I have, therefore, included wherever possible direct quotes which illustrate the human realities behind the figures.

The workers' job expectations

Since *The Affluent Worker* study by Goldthorpe and his colleagues, it has been accepted by most industrial sociologists that the objective qualities of the work itself do not determine the experiences of the worker at work. Workers doing identical jobs may have very different experiences, depending on the expectations which they bring to their work. This is especially so at a place like Saint Theresa's, where people come from very different cultural backgrounds and age groups.

In order to assess people's expectations, during the structured interviews, staff were shown a list of nine attributes of work and asked to say which three they regarded as most important in decreasing order of importance. After appropriate weighting, job security and good workmates emerged as clear favourites in the entire sample, with working conditions and interest and variety coming next. These preferences, however, conceal significant variations among the different groups in the sample, as shown in Table 1.3. Portering and dining-room staff expressed a preference for working conditions, job security and workmates. By contrast, white-collar and cooking staff expressed a clear preference for intrinsic aspects of the job (interest, pride) and a career. This trend would have been even more pronounced, if all five older unqualified cooks had not placed 'job security' at the top of their list of priorities.

Several things must be noted in connection with workers' priorities regarding their jobs. First of all, these priorities should not be seen as 'prior orientations' that the worker forms outside the workplace and then brings into the workplace. On the contrary, the work experience itself influences and shapes these expectations and vice versa, the expectations influence the actual experience during the work day. In answering this question, many people said 'Now,

TABLE 1.3
Top four work priorities of staff at Saint Theresa's

	M	C	KP	TP	D	All
Interest and variety	2	2				3=
Pride in the product	1=					
Career in catering	1=	3				
Helping others						
Good workmates	4		1	1=	2	1=
Good working conditions		4	4=	4	1	3=
Good supervision			3			
Good pay and overtime			2	3	3	
Job security		1	4=	1=	4	1=

M : Management and office staff
C : Cooks (all grades)
KP : Kitchen-porters
TP : Trolley-porters
D : Dining-room staff including supervisors

1: Top priority; 2: Second priority; etc.; =: Equal placing

Note: This table was constructed by assigning a weight of 3 to each respondent's first priority, 2 to their second and 1 to their third, and then aggregating across each group.

let's see, what does my job have? Career? No. Interest? No. I suppose, working conditions are decent, they are important for me ...', etc. Alternatively, some people placed at the top of their list of expectations something they felt *was missing* in their work. Rubina, 19, is an assistant cook who studies for her catering qualifications on a day-release:

> The work here is slapdash; you are in such a hurry you can't put the finishing touches. It's not up to restaurant standard; it doesn't bring out your best qualities, unless you work for a function. For me, pride in what I do, that's the most important thing.

The high emphasis placed on pay by portering and dining-room staff does not mean that these workers are 'instrumentally motivated', that the job is only a means towards money in the sense used by Goldthorpe et al. (1968:160ff). In fact, nothing would be further from the truth. Those groups for which pay is an important priority reported that good workmates are an even higher priority. Any stereotypes of money-motivated workers as individualistic and unconcerned about the quality of their jobs do not seem to apply to workers at Saint Theresa's. Many of them saw money as the only possible reason for holding on to jobs with little else to offer. In response to the question 'What keeps you here?' 25 out of 53 manual workers answered either 'The money' or 'It's just a job' and 4 said that they were 'used' to the place. 24 out of 34 portering and dining-room staff gave answers to this effect.

Mrs Maria Romano, a Portuguese catering assistant of 15 years service, for example, said:

> What keeps me here? Sometimes I ask myself this question. It's partly my difficulty with English. I am fed up with management and some people here, but I am afraid to move jobs. Sometimes I don't know why I waste myself here. Money is bad, management is bad. But I don't like changing jobs. Here I know who is good and who is bad. I also want to be near my husband who also works here. And, of course, I need the money.

Similar views were expressed by many other workers, including Mrs McBain, a West Indian dining-room assistant in her late 50s:

> You need the money, you need the work. I prefer to stay in one place. I don't want to leave here after all these years. Besides, where can I go?

It would be a travesty to regard workers like them as 'instrumentally oriented'. The notion that expectations somehow determine the workers' choice of a job seems totally misplaced; the very concept of choice is alien to the universe of many workers. Nichols' and Beynon's account of worker attitudes in the chemical industry could be an apt description of the 'catering trap' as experienced by many workers at Saint Theresa's:

> 'stuck' and 'have to'; this is the language of working-class freedom. 'You're trapped in this job. Every man in this plant is trapped here, believe it or not. It might seem strange to you, but everyone here *is* trapped. You've got to stay whether you like it or not.' (Nichols and Beynon, 1977:28)

While such views were expressed by most of the ancillary (portering and dining-room) workers, a very different picture prevailed among white-collar staff and kitchen staff. Only 5 of the 34 ancillary staff said that the reason for staying in their job was that they liked it or some aspect of it; 2 of these were catering supervisors and 1 was the storeroom supervisor (who has been included in the group of the kitchen-porters for the purposes of the sample).

In contrast to the views of the ancillary workers, all 6 clerical and junior management staff and 11 out of the 19 cooks responded to the question 'What keeps you here?' by saying that they *liked* an aspect of the job or the job as a whole. Mr Sprake, the assistant manager in charge of the kitchen:

> Working in catering is most satisfying because you see the result of your efforts. It is a practical job, a challenging job. Also my colleagues here, we work together very successfully. But above all, I get job satisfaction, very much so.

Barbara, an Italian assistant head-cook, who had worked at Saint Theresa's since 1964 and was in charge of the diet kitchen:

> I love this hospital, I like cooking *for patients*. Everyone works for money, but it is not enough.

Nick, a young trainee cook, about to appear on a television competition for young chefs:

> I love the job! There is variety, it's interesting. I enjoy doing it, that's what keeps me here.

Several did have a more instrumental attitude, seeing their job as a step towards a career in catering or towards opening their own restaurant. Andrew, a young assistant head-cook, who already possessed several catering qualifications and preferred calling himself 'a chef' rather than 'a cook':

> I am still learning, but I may leave here in the next six months and try and move up the scale. I want to keep moving upwards, become a head-chef and then move to management.

These views come from a different world from the world of the ancillary workers whose answers were mostly 'You can't get jobs elsewhere. You need the money, you need the job.' The answers of clerical, management and most cooking staff come from the confident world of choices, of careers, of plans. It is not just that the reasons for staying in their jobs are different, but that positive reasons are offered rather the lack of choice. Whether each and every one of these people genuinely had many choices is not the crucial thing. The important division is between people who thought they had a choice and those who, for a wide variety of reasons, did not. This influenced many of the other attitudes and feelings of the individuals in my sample, towards their job, their fellow workers and management.

Above all it influenced the extent of their job satisfaction. (See Table 1.4c) Those who felt that they had choices enjoyed the positive aspects of their work and largely put up with the negative ones. The degree of job satisfaction depended on the balance between the two. For those for whom the job was just a job the positive aspects of their work were mere consolations, which made work bearable. What coloured their attitudes and experiences was the fact that they did a job which they fundamentally did not want – a job which violated their personality and wishes. Jose-Luis Suarez, a trolley-porter who had worked at Saint Theresa's since the late 1960s, was married to one of the dining-room assistants. He talked to me at length about his life and work:

> You work like a machine here. You do what they tell you. You work for eight hours, you go home and that's it. Respect for each other is the most important thing and is lacking here. People are demoralized, especially the older people. Many times I feel depressed, I do my eight hours here, go home and try to forget about it. Still, I like the job, otherwise I wouldn't be here; but the things you see depress you. I am more serious now; before I was more cheerful. Most of my friends have left and I have stopped seeing them.

The depth, complexity and ambivalence of such a response illustrate the difficulties in obtaining accurate and reliable measures of job satisfaction. Answers to direct questions such as 'How satisfied are you with your job?' are notoriously unreliable. It is always preferable to compare one job to another one, a previous one for instance, or to some common standard. Unfortunately, given the varied backgrounds of workers at Saint Theresa's and their different lengths of service it was not possible to ask such comparative questions. Instead, after they had listed their priorities with regard to their job, I asked them: '*As far as these important things are concerned* would you say that your present job is first rate, pretty good, so-so, not too good or very bad?' On a few occasions, especially when interviewing foreign staff, I had to discuss at some length their views before they decided how they should answer.

The answers, as outlined in Tables 1.4a and 1.4b, reveal a consistent pattern. The vast majority of white-collar staff and cooks

TABLE 1.4a
Evaluation of own job by staff at Saint Theresa's

	M	C	KP	TP	D	All
First rate	2	2 (1)	1 (*)	0	1	6 (1)
Pretty good	3	13 (5)	1	2	5 (2)	24 (7)
So-so	0	1	6 (3)	3 (2)	6 (2)	16 (7)
Not too good	1	2	2 (1)	1	3 (1)	9 (2)
Very bad	0	1	0	1 (1)	2 (2)	4 (3)
TOTAL	6	19 (6)	10 (4)	7 (3)	17 (7)	59 (20)

Note: Foreign workers' responses in parentheses.

(*) the store-house supervisor

- M : Management and office staff
- C : Cooks (all grades)
- KP : Kitchen-porters
- TP : Trolley-porters
- D : Dining-room staff including supervisors

TABLE 1.4b
Evaluation of own job by staff with more than 4 years' service at Saint Theresa's

	M	C	KP	TP	D	All
First rate	0	1	1	0	1	3
Pretty good	0	6	0	0	1	7
So-so	0	0	2	2	5	9
Not too good	0	0	0	1	3	4
Very bad	0	0	0	1	2	3
TOTAL	0	7	3	4	12	26

TABLE 1.4c
Evaluation of own job by staff against responses to the question 'What keeps you in this job?'

	First rate	Pretty good	So-so	Not too good	Very bad
What keeps you in this job?					
Money/it's a job	0	7	8	8	3
Enjoy/like job etc.	6	10	3	0	0
I am used to it	0	1	2	0	1
Career	0	4	0	1	0
Others (friends, location, etc.)	0	2	3	0	0
TOTAL	6	24	16	9	4

claimed that their job was either first rate or pretty good. The portering and dining-room staff, however, had a far more negative response with 15 out of 34 seeing their job as about average and 9 as bad; indeed, excepting the storekeeper and the dining-room supervisors, all of the older and all of the foreign staff in these sections saw their jobs as average or worse.

The kitchen

Tables 1.4a and 1.4b indicate that very different feelings prevailed among cooking staff from those of dining-room and portering workers. In sharp contrast to complaints coming from 'unskilled' staff, the cooks of all grades at Saint Theresa's reported a substantial degree of satisfaction. 15 out of 19, including all of the older and foreign staff, saw their jobs as 'pretty good' or better and only 3 as 'not too good' or 'very bad'. It should be kept in mind that 11 out of the 19 cooks had less than 2 years' service at Saint Theresa's and came straight from college; all of these younger cooks were British and chose catering 'as a career'. Six of the remaining 8 cooks were foreign, having an average of 15 years' service.

To what extent were the differences in job satisfaction between the cooks and the remaining workers due to objective differences in the jobs themselves? Did the cooks enjoy greater autonomy and control on the job, did they have greater freedom and responsibility? In order to determine some of the objective qualities of people's work a Job Index was constructed on the basis of answers to 9 questions as shown in Table 1.5. These questions concerned the degree of autonomy as well as the prospects afforded by each job.

The index is a standard-type additive one based on trichotomies. Affirmative answers scored 1 point, negative ones scored 3 points and residual answers (like 'Sometimes' or 'It depends') scored 2 points. A person answering all the questions affirmatively would score 9 points, while one answering all of them negatively would score 27 points. (In the actual interviews, some of the questions were phrased so that an affirmative answer scored 3 points and a negative one 1 point.) The items were chosen as much as possible to be 'of the same type', but there is no denying that there is an ad hoc quality about them. At the same time, the index provides a method of relating large amounts of data in a relatively simple manner.[3]

TABLE 1.5
Items on the Job Index

1. The job is routine, the same day in day out.
2. In my job I work too fast most of the time.
3. I am tired at the end of each day.
4. My job is too simple to bring out my best qualities.
5. My job gives me no chance to try out my own ideas.
6. I can do my job and keep my mind on other things.
7. My job is not important for the success of this organization.
8. My job does not lead to promotion, no matter how well I do it.
9. There are no short-cuts to make my job easier.

TABLE 1.6
Average Job Index scores at Saint Theresa's

Management and office staff:	20.8
Cooks (all grades):	18.6
Kitchen-porters:	16.2
Trolley-porters:	13.0
Dining-room staff (including supervisors):	14.6

High scores indicate a high level of job autonomy (27 = max score)
Low scores indicate a low level of job autonomy (9 = min score)

Table 1.6 indicates a substantial difference in the Job Index scores of the different groups at Saint Theresa's. Kitchen staff, both cooks *and* kitchen-porters scored significantly higher than dining-room staff and trolley-porters. The result is entirely consistent with the 'craft organization' of the kitchen, which allowed considerable autonomy to cooks and even kitchen-porters. Although kitchen staff operated to a menu, recipe books were rarely used at Saint Theresa's: instead kitchen staff used their judgment, experience and skill in preparing the meals, in judging the quantities of the different ingredients and the times of cooking. Improvisation was not discouraged by management, who had deliberately reduced the amount of convenience and processed foods used. 'They have much greater responsibility now,' I was told by Mr Sprake, who added that 'before [the changes] they used to work as if on an assembly line, mechanically, lacking control; we are now using much more fresh food, fresh vegetables and they can use their skills to a greater extent.' These views were echoed by kitchen staff and I was able to confirm them through observation.

In the well-ventilated, well-illuminated kitchen on the fourth floor, five or six work-groups worked, one each on the main courses, one on vegetables and one on desserts. The size of these work-groups varied from 2 (a cook and a kitchen-porter) to 5 and the complexity of their task varied too. The menu specified the main items to be cooked each day, but at the start of the day decisions had to be taken – if several staff were absent, the menu was simplified. 'Some days I expect two men to do the job of four staff. But you can't ask two men to do the job of ten men,' said Mr Sprake, the assistant manager responsible for the kitchen. Staff were allocated to their work-groups by the two head-cooks, although he had a say on who worked with whom.

Cooking at Saint Theresa's was remarkably similar to home-cooking on a large scale. There was no overall plan or standard procedures. Highly skilled cooking could frequently be seen side by side with mechanical preparation of convenience food. On one day, 600 fish and chips portions were cooked for patients and a further 400 for hospital staff. Fish was delivered on the day already cut and boned, but staff prepared their own batter (scorning the batter mixes commonly used by fish and chips outlets). Both frozen and fresh potatoes were used for chips, depending on the number of staff available; on that particular day because of the large amounts of cooking involved, frozen chips were preferred. One of the head-cooks was in overall charge of frying, which started at 10.30 and lasted for two hours.

A second work-team, headed by an assistant head-cook, was cooking 200 portions of poached fish. White sauce was prepared without so much as weighing a single ingredient; if, as it happened, there was some extra, it was placed in the refrigerator for use in some other dish the next day. On the same day, Nick, the apprentice cook about to appear on TV, worked with a kitchen-porter preparing 100 Scotch eggs, using fresh eggs and sausage meat, to be fried in the afternoon, after the frying of the fish had finished. A separate work-group prepared the vegetables, all of which, except peas, were fresh.

On the same day, three young women cooks were preparing sandwiches and canapés for 122 participants of a nursing seminar, taking place at the hospital. They were allowed to choose the ingredients, which included 'exotic' ones, like green, yellow and red pimentoes, olives, asparagus and artichoke hearts; they obviously took great pride in the quality and the appearance of their product and invited the other cooks to have a look. Amidst all this creative activity, however, some short-cut cooking did occur; in the pastry kitchen, Manolis, an assistant head-cook, aided occasionally by a kitchen-porter, was making several trays of lemon-pie, using a large number of packets of a well-known commercial brand.

This juxtaposition of convenience cooking and highly skilled cooking was a regular feature of the kitchen at Saint Theresa's. Flexibility was the rule of the day. On the particular day described above, Rodrigo, who had started fourteen years earlier as a kitchen-porter, eventually becoming one of the two head-cooks, said:

> Each day is different. It depends on the number of staff we have, on the menu and on the functions. Today is a very busy day – people have to work very hard. But you don't expect a person to sweat every day.

Earlier that day, I saw Mr Gorman, the district catering manager, and Mr Sprake busily preparing and dishing out Russian salad for another function, a lunchtime party for physicians. In the evening, George, the most highly regarded of the assistant head-chefs, and three other cooks prepared a three-course meal, including roast beef, for a retirement party of 100. They were all, of course, working overtime. Courses for the different functions were selected from a menu of over one hundred items 'which would grace any haute-cuisine restaurant', in Mr Gorman's words.

Cooking at Saint Theresa's allowed plenty of room for talent, individual creativity and skill. Many of the cooks, like Nick, Andrew and George, exhibited precisely these qualities. Like a good house-cook, Saint Theresa's cooks never threw away meat bones without first extracting stock, nor did they thicken a sauce by merely adding flour. Meat was always quickly fried before being stewed, and the salt was added at the correct moment. Delicate cooking touches abounded, the slice of lemon with the boiling potatoes, the genuine broth for the stew, the capers for the Russian salad.

These cooks took great pride in their work and cared for the final product. Sixteen out of 19 cooks saw that their jobs as skilled or very skilled. The same number thought that the quality of the meals they prepared was good or very good. Fifteen of them said that they enjoyed cooking as an activity. A lot of them expressed concern that the food did not reach the patients and the dining-rooms in the condition that it left the kitchen and many complained about the lack of feedback and recognition; Gill, a young and disillusioned cook, had come from Sunderland to take up her job at Saint Theresa's three years earlier:

> You have to feel that you are doing something good; here you don't see the finished product in the wards, how it is presented. You get no feedback from the patients either, so there is less job satisfaction than working in a restaurant.

And Angela from Lincolnshire who had started at the same time:

> Everyone has to do the same task, the same way, except when you work in the diet kitchen. It would be nice to be allowed to put your own touches.

These complaints frequently revealed the very different amounts of autonomy that different cooks at Saint Theresa's enjoyed – with some of them generally restricted to the more mundane tasks and never entrusted with cooking for a prestigious function. They also reveal the high standards of the cooks themselves while cooking at an average cost of £1.10 per patient per day. No fewer than 6 had long-term plans of opening and running their own restaurants, 7 would like to become head-chefs and 3 saw their future in catering management.

Some cooks did have deeper grievances about their work; Diane, a black trainee cook, for instance, complained about management and supervision. In response to my question whether she controlled the machines or felt controlled by them, she said 'I *am* the machine' and added:

> There is no art in cooking for the NHS. You are not allowed to do anything, can't talk to anybody, can't laugh or smile, can't go to the loo even.

In spite of grievances like these, however, a very substantial majority of cooking staff, 15 out of 19, were satisfied with their job. This was undoubtedly due in part to the jobs themselves. In terms of job autonomy and in terms of expectations and ambitions, the cooks were something of an aristocracy of labour at Saint Theresa's. All but 3 of them found their job interesting all the time or most of the time. Only 4 of them thought that the job was 'too simple to bring out their best qualities'. Finally the majority reported a variety of 'short-cuts' and 'games' which they used to liven up their work, to make it easier and to impart their own character to it. Andrew:

> There are short-cuts in every job. You constantly pick up tricks from those who've been here longer; you also work out your own ways of doing things. The longer you stay here, the more

you can do your own thing, but some of the short-cuts lower the quality.

Most of the cooks saw their jobs as well as their future in terms of *choices*. Although the amount of control available to each person varied considerably, most of them felt that they had some control over their work and over their lives.

The porters and the dining-room staff

The same was not true for the majority of dining-room staff and porters. As was seen earlier, 23 out of 34 such workers regarded their job as 'just a job', in a period when jobs are not easy to come by. Only 3 said that they liked their job or some aspect of their job in response to the question 'What keeps you here?' Nearly all of them saw their jobs as unskilled and a substantial proportion said that they found their jobs boring and monotonous, as shown from Table 1.7.[4]

TABLE 1.7
How interesting were their own jobs

	M	C	KP	TP	D	All
Interesting all the time	4	3	0	1	1	9
Interesting most of the time	2	13	6	2	12	35
Fairly dull and monotonous	0	3	3	0	1	7
Very dull and monotonous	0	0	1	4	3	8
TOTALS	6	19	10	7	17	59

M : Management and office staff
C : Cooks (all grades)
KP : Kitchen–porters
TP : Trolley-porters
D : Dining-room staff including supervisors

Porters generally found their jobs less interesting than cooks; and trolley-porters found their jobs less interesting than kitchen-porters. Kitchen-porters enjoyed some of the greater autonomy which prevailed in the kitchen and their Job Index (16.2) is a lot higher than that of the trolley-porters (13.0). Some of the kitchen-porters, having served in the kitchen for several years, were quite skilled cooks in their own right and were given considerable freedom in their work. The skills picked up by the older kitchen-porters made them resent some of the younger assistant cooks, who enjoyed superior status and privileges. Diego, a trained plasterer in Spain, had come to Britain in the 1960s and after different hotel jobs had been a kitchen-porter since 1969. He had lately developed butchery skills and was now in charge of cutting meat:

> Younger cooks come and ask: 'How do you do this, Diego, how do you do that?' Sometimes I get very upset and I tell them 'You are cook, you know what you do.'

Kitchen-porters spent some of their time in food preparation and some in washing up, some under direct supervision, some alone. This creates some conflict over who gets the 'gravy jobs'; and as the same individuals are constantly landed with the 'stinkers', allegations of favouritism were rife.[5] Morgan, a Scot well-known for his radical beliefs which included 'I hate *all* management', said:

> You keep on washing up and they keep on bringing you more. Day in day out, I hardly do anything else.

Washing up at St Theresa's is massive. Due to the relatively primitive catering technology employed, there are large numbers of pots, pans, trays and cooking utensils of all sorts which constantly need washing. At the time of my visit, the dish-washing machine was not working and two kitchen-porters, in Wellington boots standing in several inches of water, tried to keep pace with the constantly mounting pile of washing up, in a room adjoining the kitchen. Morgan and Jimmy, the diminutive Scot and the exuberant West Indian, made an unlikely duo, but their views were in total harmony.

> JIMMY: The job is bad, but management makes it really nasty.
> MORGAN: No management should ever be in the kitchen. Before the changes things ran very smoothly with Patty [the head-cook]. We did the same amount of work without anyone breathing down our neck.

The trolley-porters found their jobs even less interesting than the kitchen-porters. Twice every day an armada of 35 trolleys leave the kitchen loaded with meals and desserts for the patients. They are taken by the trolley-porters to the different wards, some of which are several hundred yards away. They are each supposed to take one trolley but they in fact always take two; this cuts the number of trips they have to make to 3 or 4. Management has repeatedly tried to stop this practice, but it has been to no avail – at the time of my visit, they issued a memorandum stating that they would accept no responsibility in the event of an accident.

The trolley-porters are rarely visited by management. Vassilis, a Cypriot porter of very long service, is supposed to supervise them and to ensure that food which is returned from the wards is in fact thrown away; his job title is charge-hand, but he considers himself a porter. He came from Cyprus in the 1950s – his father had had an operation at Saint Theresa's, and when the money ran out Vassilis was forced to take up the first job that he could to support the rest of his family. He started as a trolley-porter on 28 March 1957 – like conscripted and convicted men, the older workers at Saint Theresa's remember exactly the day it all started. After 27 years of service, Vassilis looks much older than his 56 years. Five or 6 of the trolley-porters are young English men in their teens and early twenties and the rest are foreign men in their forties or fifties, all of them having served the hospital for many years. Their relationship with Vassilis is hardly one between supervised and supervisor. They spend a lot of time together, especially in between mealtimes, in a room allocated to them. It is a small, windowless room, but it is their territory, the men's room. It is not decorated with pin-ups, but with four small canvases painted by someone who left a few years earlier. Listening to the radio, playing cards, having a laugh and a smoke, time passes before the next round.

Apart from the relative freedom from supervision, trolley-porters had traditionally seen petty pilfering as a fringe benefit of their job; Mr Rocha, one of the longest-serving porters, said:

> Whole chickens used to disappear between the kitchen and the wards. And why not? What else was there in this job? Then with the changes, management put the screws on. They shouldn't have squeezed so suddenly, so completely, people had families to support. . . . Then after the changes, many of the porters left, some of them pretended to be sick. They are now employing a lot of English youngsters; they do not work hard, they are not used to hard work, but they can accept the rota and the conditions of work.

If portering is a man's job, waitressing at Saint Theresa's is strictly a woman's. However, the same complex mix of nationalities could be found among the women working in the dining-rooms. Three of those I interviewed had husbands working as porters, and several had been in the hospital for many years. Most of the women worked in the two large dining-rooms, where a new system of self-service had been installed by management to replace the old cafeteria. Customers helped themselves from rotating hot platforms, the giro-sells, each carrying five or six full plates, designed to keep the food hot. The catering assistants served behind a counter, dishing out the food on to plates and constantly replenishing the heated carousels. Maria Carillo:

> Working conditions are very bad. The giro-sells make me more tired; you get too hot, summer and winter. Sometimes I nearly faint from tiredness and heat, standing up all the time. Once Miss Jenkins [Assistant Manager] told me off for sitting down; she said that next time she would report me to Miss Summerfield.

Working on the giro-sells was recognized as the worst job, because of the heat, the pressure and the constant supervision. By contrast, working in the nurses' or the physicians' dining-room was seen as a 'gravy job'. As with the kitchen-porters, the distribution of good and bad jobs was a cause of deep resentment, especially as it fuelled feelings of racial discrimination. Maria Romano, whose husband was a trolley-porter, was 'fed up' earning £57 net, after 15 years of service. She did some cashiering, but most of her time was spent on the hated giro-sells:

> Work is too hard, but if you complain they make your life harder. If you say you don't feel well they show no consideration or respect. Not all the girls work on the giro-sells but I am asked to work there very often. They have ways of making your life harder if you complain. A lot of the older staff, all foreign, left because they got fed up. To begin with English girls didn't stay here long, but now they do, especially as they get better treatment than foreign staff.

Like porters, dining-room staff experienced low overall job satisfaction, some of them verging on despair. Maria Romano, Maria Carillo and Nora Suarez were probably the most deeply unhappy individuals I interviewed in any establishment. Few, however, felt bored, and the majority (as shown in Table 7), found their jobs interesting most of the time. However, as I was told again and again, 'it is the people which make the job interesting.'

Managers realized that the jobs in the dining-room were, in Miss

Summerfield's words, 'mundane, the same thing day after day'. Miss Jenkins, the assistant manager responsible for the dining-areas, was dynamic and self-confident; after two years on the job, she was very outspoken about her staff, most of whom were 20 years older than her:

> Although people with qualifications do apply, the majority of the ones we employ in the dining areas have no qualifications or a few CSEs. They have to be 'reliable' people, with low aspirations as it is a pretty monotonous job down there. They don't see it as a career, more as a job. . . . Money is their only motivation, money-grabbers some of them, I think.

Money and grievances

As shown in Table 1.2, for most of these workers the job was merely a way of earning a living, of supporting themselves and their families. What, then, were the working conditions and the pay of these workers? As most of these workers worked on a roster, working on average 2 weekends out of 3, their wage packet varied from week to week considerably, depending on the amount of weekend work and late nights.

While almost all workers worked a basic 40-hour week, some put in substantial amounts of overtime, especially if they were involved in functions. For these reasons, a maximum and a minimum figure

TABLE 1.8
Gross and take-home pay of workers at Saint Theresa's

	Gross for 40 hrs	Take-home Maximum	Minimum
Cooks	80.63 (*)	92	71
Kitchen-porters	70.03	78	64
Trolley-porters	70.03	88	61
Dining-room staff	68.98–82.38	69	57

(*) Cooks, Grade 7

Note: All figures in £; the wages of the trainee cooks, the storeman and the charge-hand are not included above. The range given for dining-room staff applies to all staff, from catering assistant to senior dining-room supervisor. London weighting of £15.29 per week for all grades is not included. All figures applied to 1984.

was recorded for each employee's take-home pay. The results as shown in Table 1.8 confirm the view that catering workers are near the bottom of the wage league. A junior cook's typical earnings of £1.99 per hour, at a time when the hourly average for all manual workers was £3.26 and for cooks £2.75, would place him in the bottom 5 per cent of all male manual workers. A typical kitchen-porter at Saint Theresa's, earning £102 for a 40-hour week, including two out of three weekends, would be in the bottom 10 per cent of all male manual workers, in spite of his weekend and shift-work bonuses and London allowance. A catering assistant on gross weekly wages of £68.98 would be in the bottom 10 per cent of all female workers and in the bottom 25 per cent of all manual female workers.[6] Virtually all of the workers in my sample would be included in the 'low pay' category, whichever definition one may chose to adopt.[7] They were all earning less than the TUC's definition of low pay which stood at £100 per week for full-time and £2.60 per hour for part-time staff.

In spite of the low level of wages, only 9 of the 34 ancillary staff saw it as a cause of dissatisfaction and only 4 as the main problem with their job. (See Table 1.9.) 'The pay is all right considering the economic situation, although it is not enough for a decent living,' I was told by Juan, a Filipino kitchen-porter, supporting his wife, his sister and his young son on between £66 and £90 per week. His response was quite typical, and suggests that the government's assault on expectations has not been unsuccessful. And Mr Gorman: 'People's attitudes have changed for the better – they have a job

TABLE 1.9
'The main problem with my job is ...'

	C	P	D	All
Bad pay	2	2	2	6
Management or supervision	4	5	8	17
The job itself	3	4	3	10
The hours/rosters	2	2	2	6
None	5	2	2	9
Others (including unions, location, no prospects)	3	2	0	5
TOTAL	19	17	17	53

C: cooks;   P: porters;   D: dining-room staff

and want to keep it.' While many of his staff would dispute that their attitude was 'better', few of the ancillary workers would dispute the second part of his statement.

Workers and management at Saint Theresa's

Management at Saint Theresa's were not in an enviable position. They had inherited an extremely inefficient operation, with little control and little discipline. When Mr Gorman, the district catering manager, had taken over, he had made it clear that important changes would have to be made and he wanted managers capable of seeing them through. Miss Summerfield:

> We [managers] all had to re-apply for our jobs. It was very demoralizing and disillusioning. More recently, the threat of privatization has brought even worse problems. Everybody's job seems at risk, not just management but also staff.

Before 1980, there was no rostering system and workers clocked on enormous amounts of overtime, liberally allocated by the kitchen and dining-room superintendents, who had been 'one of the lads'. Patty Hughes had been the head-cook or kitchen superintendent for fifteen years; many of the older people spoke affectionately of the good old days, before the appointment of Mr Sprake, when she was in charge. She, however, preferred having a manager in the kitchen:

> Before the 'changes' people didn't want to work and I had to do their job. The union ruled the kitchen and it was hard to be on top. There was no discipline, no hard work. Cooks show more responsibility now; you need a tough man to make them do anything.

And there can be little doubt that Mr Sprake was precisely that, a tough man. He had undoubtedly been the iron will behind the changes. A man who did not mince his words, he talked to me at length and with pride about his job and the improvements he had implemented. In less than four years he had developed and introduced a new rostering system, which meant that people never having worked shift-work before were asked to do so. New job descriptions were prepared allowing flexibility and mobility in the staffing levels and work practices. Control over supplies was tightened and a manager was present at all times, including weekends. His description of the changes has a journalistic precision:

> We approached the union with our package but they came back with a blanket 'No'. We then decided to go ahead and offered the new terms to the staff. There was a one-week sympathetic strike in support of porters who were facing a similar rationalization, but support for the strike was not whole-hearted and we managed to keep a service going. Then there was an eight-week overtime ban, when we [management] had to do many of the basic duties. It was then that we really found out how long it takes to scrub a kitchen floor, to deliver milk or to carry a trolley to the ward. It was then that we really learned the tricks of the trade. But the overtime ban was hurting the staff more than us and in the end, they were defeated. After a variety of stalling tactics the changes were implemented virtually unchanged in November 1982.

In his view, a majority of his staff had come to accept the changes while most of those who could not move with the times had left, to be replaced by the new breed of staff. Only a few of the old guard remained resentful.

> For them, I represent the transition from an easy life to a hard life for four or five individuals, who are waging a war of sorts.

Mr Sprake's outspoken, direct and determined style of management is representative of what has been nicknamed 'macho-management'. This is the management which does not shy away from confrontation with the unions and has little patience for the politics of negotiation and compromise (Purcell, 1982). His views are unequivocal, precise and to the point:

> We are very strict. . . . The rules are very strict – the length of the breaks, clocking in, smoking, litter and so on. . . . I feel strongly and a bit bitter about union activity. My experience with unions is that they don't care about service but about themselves.

Unlike the older staff, however, many of the younger cooks did not object to Mr Sprake's style of management. Many of them found him considerate and helpful. Twelve out of 17 cooks said that he was 'friendly and informal', as shown in Table 1.10, although 5 of those thought it necessary to add some other adjective, such as

TABLE 1.10
Staff attitudes towards management

	C	KP	TP	D	All
My manager is:					
friendly and informal	12	3	2	7	24
formal and impersonal	1	1	1	1	4
correct but unfriendly	3	3	3	1	10
pushy and bossy	3	3	1	8	15
TOTAL	19	10	7	17	53
Management is					
doing a good job	13	5	3	6	27
not doing a good job	4	2	4	8	18
don't know	2	3	0	3	8
TOTAL	19	10	7	17	53
Managers are arrogant to their staff					
disagree	13	5	5	8	31
agree	3	4	2	9	18
don't know	3	1	0	0	4
TOTAL	19	10	7	17	53

C : Cooks (all grades)
KP : Kitchen-porters
TP : Trolley-porters
D : Dining-room staff including supervisors

'and pushy too', or 'and crafty'. To be sure, some of the cooks felt a deep bitterness towards management, and towards Mr Sprake in particular. Diane:

> I am not one of his chosen people because I don't like to lick his shoes, like the majority here. He told me that I had a bad attitude after I joined the union, and then he stopped talking to me. If I come on Monday and I am happy, by the end of the week I am depressed; he picks on small things. I call him Hitler. He doesn't like to see you talking to the union man.

In spite of such deep bitterness, however, a clear majority of the cooks seemed to get on with management, certainly much better than the rest of the staff. Several expressed admiration, although some of them had reservations especially about what they saw as favouritism. George, whose cooking skills commanded general admiration and was involved in most prestige functions had no personal complaints against management, but he said:

> Their attitude towards the staff is not too good. The chosen few syndrome. It worries me that I could lose the standing of being one of the chosen few.

The situation, however, was much worse among ancillary workers, especially older ones. Many of them had very deep resentments against specific managers, especially the younger ones, and against the 'changes'. These feelings were stronger among older, foreign staff, some of whom were positively bursting with discontent, as soon as I started talking to them. Nora Suarez, the wife of Jose-Luis, had been a catering assistant since 1969:

> The job is a lot worse now, for a lot less money, before [the changes] the job didn't kill you; now sometimes you are dead when you finish. Most managers have very bad manners, they don't even tell you 'good-morning'. For the last two years there has been trouble every day. There are all these rules, 'Don't smoke', 'Don't talk', 'Don't sit'. Mr Sprake is really nasty, but he has calmed down recently.

These views were echoed by other staff; Morgan:

> Rota and other changes have made things worse for us. We now do more late shifts; money is worse. Conditions are bad.

And Mr Carrillo, another kitchen-porter:

> It used to be 'one man one job' here; but the union is finished now. We now work 'one man one thousand jobs.' The money is also worse since the changes. Before [the changes] you did a lot of overtime and got £100 home; now wages are very low. The job too is less interesting now. Before they cared about quality. You work harder now and the conditions are worse.

Through the many criticisms of management there are several common threads, favouritism, discrimination, 'bad manners' and arrogance. Two of the older dining-room assistants:

> This is the worst time we have had in this hospital. People in management don't know how to treat people. There is favouritism and unequal treatment. They discriminate against black and foreign people. Sometimes they go past you and they

don't see you. No manners. They never say 'Girls, thank you' after a hard day's work.

English girls here can talk as much as they like, but I am not allowed to open my mouth. Since Mr Sprake came here, no foreign girls have been employed and there is a lot of discrimination against us.

The allocation of overtime was a particularly touchy subject; Mr Rocha, trolley-porter of ten years experience at the hospital:

Discrimination and favouritism is the thing that annoys me most. Overtime used to be allocated by the supervisors but this is now done by management who don't know who is a good worker. I personally earn more money now, as a result of the new rosters, because I do more weekend work. But the introduction of the new rosters happened without any consultation.

Even more widespread were feelings that managers treated their staff without respect. Many of the foreign workers complained about the 'bad manners' of management, a topic which must have been discussed frequently among themselves. As shown in Table 1.10, a substantial number of the ancillary staff thought that management sometimes treated their staff arrogantly and many thought that management were not doing a good job. Many complained about the unpredictability of certain managers, especially Mr Sprake. Norman, a young trolley-porter:

You don't know what is going through his mind. Sometimes he doesn't talk to you for no reason; or he doesn't give you overtime for no reason. Yet at other times he is quite friendly and chatty.

Most of these complaints concerned unfairness, rudeness and unpredictability. Yet, a handful of people, like Morgan, had a more political understanding of the role of management:

You are always wrong, he is always right. They don't come half-way to meet you. I'm always arguing. I don't like him. Very arrogant. You talk to people but you are not supposed to. When you write a book, say that I don't like management here. I don't like all management.

Morgan's views were echoed by Mike Robins, a trolley-porter who was the NUPE official at the hospital:

> Since the changes, discipline has been much stricter – workers are dominated by the clock. Management are arrogant with no concern for the problems of the staff. They breathe down your neck at all times; the atmosphere is never relaxed. They antagonize people and their presence causes aggravation. They don't realize that the jobs are uninteresting, the pay is low, the hours are bad, and the prospects non-existent.

In spite of the strength of these views, only 5 of the 25 staff with less than three years' service thought that management was arrogant. Of the remaining 28 staff, no fewer than 13 thought so. This may be due either to the fact that the first group had not been through the 'trauma' of the changes or that they were younger, British and more skilled in the majority; finally, it may be due to the fact that, as several of the older, foreign staff suggested, they were given preferential treatment by management. This possibility is strengthened by the numerous complaints concerning favouritism and the 'chosen few syndrome' discussed earlier. A whole mythology of favouritism had sprung up, the kitchen-porter who eventually became head-cook hardly speaking English, the cook who was given a car parking space 'right next to the cars of the doctors, with his name on it', the young dining-room assistant who was never put on the giro-sells.

Ethnic divisions, divisions by age, skill and work experience seemed to compound each other and feed feelings of favouritism and resentment. Rubina:

> Because you are female they discriminate. They touch you or pinch you and you have to put a stop to it. Some of the girls upstairs fall for the Spanish lover stereotype. Some of them go to bed with the cooks and then boast to their friends, but they pay for it later. And the rest of us pay too.

And Mr Rocha, the trolley-porter:

> We've been here longest, Carrillo, Suarez, Pappas, Charlie and a couple of others. Yet, management make life hard for us, they don't say good-morning, they don't give us overtime. The rest, the young English boys, are dirty and noisy, they don't work hard. But management treat them well, for a couple of

years anyway, while they're docile. Then they make life hard for them so that they leave and replace them with new blood.

Management had a different way of describing this process – one of the senior ones called it 'healthy labour turnover, not like in the past when people stagnated here.'

Finally, a significant number of people complained about having to pay for their own meals, especially as in the past meals for catering staff had been free or at a low price. Management view was that provision of free meals had not worked in the past, because people were greedy. Miss Jenkins:

> We tried offering them a free meal – it was a way of cutting down on petty pilfering of food that went on before we took over here. But then what happened was that people started taking the food home – they would bring a sandwich to eat here and would then argue about a potato or two. It became impossible and we had to stop the provision.

Workers felt that this was not right. Morgan's views on this were quite representative:

> You have to buy your own food, even though a lot of the food is thrown away or comes back from the wards. They don't provide anything to their staff, before we got two meals a day. Scrooge I call them.

However, several of the staff indicated that they had 'whatever is left in the kitchen' or 'whatever is sent back from the wards'. Only a handful of individuals from the catering department could ever be seen in the dining-rooms, and only 8 said that they had a hot meal there. One young porter cheekily complained that one of the bad aspects of his job was that he had got fat; some people, however, felt it undignified that they should have to 'pilfer' for their food. Miss Campbell:

> A lot of food gets thrown away and yet staff are not allowed to have any. Most people have to get it behind management's backs. People working in catering should always have a free meal. You work with food all day, it's you that makes it, it's you that serves it and yet you are not allowed to have one chip, especially if Mr Sprake is looking.

In spite, however, of such complaints, the figures in Table 10 suggest that the majority of staff had established an acceptable *modus vivendi* with management. Mrs Vickers, a middle-aged West Indian catering assistant for 15 years, had rarely ever been heard to say a word to any one. Most of her colleagues thought it unlikely that she would say anything to me. This is what she said:

> I don't trouble them, they don't trouble me. People do sometimes get into trouble; I haven't got into trouble yet. I come here to do my job. I don't need much help. My private life is my private life.

A precarious and charged equilibrium seemed to prevail much of the time, an equilibrium threatened at all times by some minor incident. On the second day of my visit at Saint Theresa's a small incident took place, whose significance only became clear later. I was walking back to the office with two of the managers, with whom I had had lunch. As we walked past the trolley room, they realized that no porters were to be seen. Suddenly, their confident air disappeared – I was dispatched to the office, while they went 'to the pub' in search for the missing men. At the time, I had not yet talked to any of the staff and the scene was the first indication of how easily the quiet surface of management control could be disturbed. The two managers returned to the office five minutes later beaming – the porters had mysteriously re-appeared.

Unions and conflict at Saint Theresa's

'Of course I belong to the union. They would walk all over you if you didn't' was quite a common response regarding union membership. The vast majority, however, added 'the union cannot win today'. Suarez, to whom I talked for several hours:

> A few years ago the union could help us in this hospital. But now the union is too weak. But it's not their fault. When the community does not agree, the union can do nothing. I don't blame the union. With the changes, the people here split, and when the people are not united management can do what they want.

> Before the changes, everyone working in the kitchen had been in the union. Since the changes, the union had lost half its members there, either because they left the hospital or because, with manage-

TABLE 1.11
Workers' attitudes towards unions at Saint Theresa's

	C	KP	TP	D	All
'We need union protection'					
Agree	15 (4)	6 (5)	6 (5)	17 (12)	44 (26)
Disagree	2	3 (1)	1	0	6 (1)
Don't know	2	1	0	0	3
TOTAL	19	10	7	17	53
'We need union help over pay and working conditions'					
Agree	14 (2)	7 (5)	7 (6)	17 (13)	45 (26)
Disagree	3	2 (1)	0	0	5 (1)
Don't know	2	1	0	0	3
TOTAL	19	10	7	17	53

Note: Figures in parentheses indicate *strong* agreement or disagreement

	C	KP	TP	D	All
'Is your union doing a good job for its members?' (Only union members asked; 31 out of 53 non-management staff)					
Agree	5	3	4	14	26
Disagree	1	1	1	0	3
Don't know	0	0	0	2	2
TOTAL	6	4	5	16	31
'Would you describe yourself as a committed trade-unionist?' ('Do you believe in what the union stands for?')					
Yes	3	3	5	13	24
No	0	1	0	3	4
Don't know	3	0	0	0	3
TOTAL	6	4	5	16	31

C : Cooks (all grades)
KP : Kitchen-porters
TP : Trolley-porters
D : Dining-room staff including supervisors

ment's encouragement, they left the union. Several told me that although they approved of unions, they disapproved of strikes as they could not afford to lose their income. Some of the younger cooks expressed views like Karen's:

> I don't really understand unions; I don't see the point. Awkward workers need unions to protect them. My pay is OK but not too good, I talk to management directly about it.

Management, following the example of Michael Edwardes at British Leyland, had encouraged direct communication with staff and held regular staff meetings; the union had decided to boycott such meetings, which were seen as undermining collective bargaining and had assumed a passive stance of non-cooperation. However, many of the cooks approved of them, and criticized the union for its negative position; Andrew:

> In this hospital the union rejected the changes without discussion, they rejected the bonus and productivity schemes without discussion; now we have no bonuses at all.

In spite of comments like these, Table 1.11 indicates that a large majority of staff at Saint Theresa's, *including most of those who did not belong to the union*, felt that they needed union protection as well as help over pay and working conditions. The only two cooks who did not think that they needed union protection happened to be two ex-members who had left the union during the bitter confrontation surrounding the changes.

Twenty-six of the 31 union members in my sample felt that their union officials were doing a good job for their members, although many qualified their answers by adding that the union could do relatively little in the face of management intransigence. Virtually everyone felt that there was not enough consultation between workers and management; only 5 of the cooks and 2 of the remaining staff thought that staff meetings provided adequate consultation. Nor did management intend them as real exercises in consultation; one manager candidly said,

> We have discussions but no consultations. Decisions are made or about to be made and then discussed. On small issues, yes there is consultation.

Most of the younger cooks accepted the view that managing is the job of managers and did not want a say in decision-making; they did, however, want better lines of communication with their superiors.

Contrary to the loss of membership in the kitchen, the union's membership in the dining-room had doubled since the changes. Only a handful of the women there were outside the union, and one of them said:

> At the moment they cannot win. Before, the trade union was heard when they made representations to management but not any more. I used to belong but not any more. I still support them when they go on strike, but I am against rallies and people going out in the streets. But sometimes they fight for a good cause.

Many of the women, however, were actively involved in union affairs, frequently demonstrating with other public sector or NHS workers or lobbying their local authority. A number of them featured prominently in an issue of the NUPE newspaper handing in a petition to a town hall official. Thirteen of the 16 union members in the dining-rooms would describe themselves as 'committed unionists'. Women at Saint Theresa's had decidedly more pro-union attitudes than men.[8]

Even in the dining-rooms, however, solidarity suffered as a result of divisions among the staff, especially the divisions between young and old, foreign and British. Some people, I was told, did not talk to each other; the word 'cliques' was mentioned more than once, both in the kitchen and in the dining-areas. Rubina:

> The kitchen is divided in groups, older chefs, young people, union, non-union. There are people who don't talk to each other, the Spanish don't talk to the Greeks, like. They don't talk to me and I'll be surprised if they talk to you.

Management had a hand at deepening divisions and they employed several tactics to this effect. Mr Sprake made this casual comment as we crossed Rubina in a corridor.

> Rubina is a good girl really, but she's got mixed up with bad company and has become difficult. I keep an eye on her and don't let her work with some of them. We've got to be careful, many of them living together in Suffolk House [hospital accommodation] tend to gang up.

Diane, Rubina's best friend, made the same point:

> He [Mr Sprake] doesn't like people having relationships or friendships; he puts people to work separately from their friends. He never lets two black girls to work together.

If keeping people from working with their friends was one method used by managers to prevent people from 'ganging up', 'getting at' and preferential treatment were even more common. Miss Campbell is one of the dining-room supervisors; she expressed tremendous commitment to her work and the hospital, but her views on management were very negative:

> They are not really fair. They show too much favouritism. That's why they get so much sickness. Their own people they treat like a syndicate, for the rest they don't care. Their bad manners and the war of nerves they set up make life very hard and at times unbearable. A few years ago, an Italian cook, . . . he killed himself in the kitchen, he couldn't take any more.

The cook's suicide was related to me by five individuals independently and it was a powerful part of the unwritten history of Saint Theresa's catering department. As with most history, however, there were different interpretations for this tragic incident. The workers blamed management, although two felt that some of the other cooks were also to blame for picking on him. Even if the cook's suicide was not directly the result of work factors (as one manager argued), it stands as a symbol of the bitterness which I encountered at Saint Theresa's. This bitterness, as was seen, frequently went back to people's behaviour during 'the changes' and came to reinforce the divisions which already existed.

The catering operation itself at Saint Theresa's, heterogeneous, fragmented and old-fashioned increased the likelihood of unequal treatment and favouritism. Management relied on what Edwards (1979) called 'simple control' to ensure that the work got done. On their own account, between half and three-quarters of their time was spent 'doing the rounds', on routine supervision. Their relations with the workers involved a substantial grey area, an area where control was unclear. The workers for much of the time enjoyed some discretion, especially the cooks and the porters. They used short-cuts in their work, they 'played games' which gave them a sense of autonomy, they engaged in various fiddles (like small pilfering of food), they bent the rules quite regularly and they could frequently bungle their work with impunity. However, the degree to which such practices were allowed varied at the discretion of management – and precisely, by allowing such practices to some individuals and some groups while denying them to others, by allowing them at some times and not at others, management could ensure at all times that opposition was divided.[9]

Moreover, the catering operation itself allowed considerable arbitrariness to managers – the allocation of overtime (which at times amounted to a third of the pay-packet, the difference between starvation wages and living wages), the assignment of prestigious functions, the distribution of 'gravy jobs' and 'stinkers', the moving of workers to different tasks and departments, gave them considerable scope for rewarding compliant workers and disadvantaging recalcitrant ones.

Apart from bitterness, the other major form which discontent took at Saint Theresa's was absenteeism. Three of the 5 managers regarded it as their major problem and, although it proved difficult to obtain reliable figures for the problem (estimates ranging from 10 to 20 per cent), its size was clear. One of the conditions of employment for NHS staff stipulates that in case of sickness they are entitled to up to three months' leave on full pay. This was clearly interpreted by many staff as a fringe benefit of the job. My visit took place in March 1984, towards the end of the financial year, and there could be little doubt that the workforce was seriously depleted; this was due in part to workers taking their remaining holiday entitlement and in part to their taking their sickness 'entitlement'. On several occasions during my visits the number of absent catering assistants was such that up to 7 'agency staff' had to be employed just to keep the dining-room going. The menu had to be simplified repeatedly in order to allow for absent cooks. Managers themselves sometimes had to prepare meals for functions due to staff shortages. During my five weeks at Saint Theresa's a dozen of the 88 staff never appeared once.

Mr Sprake explained to me how some of the foreign staff regularly 'fell ill' during visits home, stayed away from the hospital for several months and re-appeared with notes from doctors in Spanish, Italian or Greek certifying that they had been ill. This had been one of the main reasons they were reluctant to employ any more foreign staff. In addition, Mr Sprake had instituted a system of interviews following return from sickness and a system of check-ups by the hospital's Occupational Health Department. In spite of these measures, however, the problem remained. The new procedure of self-certification led to the one-day-off syndrome, according to Mr Sprake.

In view of the union's inability to engage in meaningful negotiations with management, in view of the divisions among the workers and in view of the low morale of certain groups of workers, this chronic absenteeism was not surprising. For the rest, discontent was choked; it turned not to anger but to bitterness and sadness, as expressed by a young woman:

> The job could be OK here if you had a supervisor you could communicate with. But not with Mr Sprake. If I had my own business and he came to ask for a job from me I would give him one, just to make him ask 'Why did I do this to them?'

What about management at Saint Theresa's? Virtually all of them felt extremely satisfied with their work; not merely had they survived a crisis, but had succeeded in eradicating restrictive practices and traditions and establishing some discipline in a workforce spoiled by years of tolerant or, as they put it, indulgent management. They had introduced a roster which precluded the possibility of staff clocking 20 or 30 hours overtime per week, as they had been known to do previously, they had re-introduced cooking with fresh ingredients and maintained a high standard of ordinary meals and an excellent standard of catering for special functions. At a time of increasing attacks on hospital catering, they provided healthy and varied meals to patients on £1.10 per day and the immediate threat of privatization had been removed. In fact Mr Sprake said:

> The degree of job satisfaction has declined for me in the last six months. As the problems become less, the job has become more boring.

Managing at Saint Theresa's was not a job for the faint-hearted. Working under constant pressure, the managers had to be resourceful and determined. Most of them approached the daily problems of their job as challenges and did not shy away from confrontation. Miss McTigue, however, the most junior manager recruited only six months previously after a stint at a West End hotel, found the pressure and the stress distressing:

> The International Hotel was a very friendly place, the atmosphere was relaxed. Here it is like an army; if you forget a packet of biscuits there is total outrage. . . . The office staff

are very very nice; they have been very helpful to me, unlike the other managers who never gave me any advice. I couldn't imagine seeing them socially outside the workplace, they are cold and impersonal. They just *don't care*.

Conclusions

Absenteeism and bitterness, then, were the costs that management had had to pay for introducing their programme of changes. That they had succeeded was in part due to their determination, single-mindedness and ability and in part to the workers' inability to present a united front. In a period of acute job shortages, when the predicament facing a middle-aged foreign worker without a job is the certainty of unemployment, management can easily exploit such divisions and impose a stricter regime of discipline. Some of their staff had accepted the necessity for this new regime, some not.

What became clear very soon was that for most ancillary workers and for some of the older cooks, the jobs at Saint Theresa's had become prisons. 'Trapped in a job' and 'The Catering Trap' were suggested to me as possible titles for this book by some of the workers who saw no alternative to their job other than the dole. They felt trapped in their job because they lacked specialized training, or because their command of English was limited, or simply because of their age, nationality and background. 'This is a very very bad job but I like to stay in the same place,' said a foreign catering assistant, who, like several others, admitted that she wouldn't know how to go about getting another job.

Leaving Saint Theresa's willingly or unwillingly was for many of these workers an extremely frightening prospect. A few years before my visit, all dining-room staff and all trolley-porters were foreign. The ones who had had enough had left; the ones who had stayed were the ones who found the prospect of leaving most frightening. Only 7 out of 34 ancillary staff admitted that they had thought of leaving their job at Saint Theresa's, but 5 of them added that they didn't think it realistic.

By contrast, most of the cooks *had* considered the possibility and expected to move to another job sooner or later. For them the jobs offered not only experience and career opportunity but also intrinsic satisfaction; having no families to support, no obligations at home, they found both the rosters and the relatively low wages quite acceptable. Far from feeling trapped in their job, most of them felt in control and derived a sense of pride and achievement from their work. To be sure, some found the discipline too demanding but even they felt that they could leave as soon as they got what they wanted from their jobs.

My principal impression from Saint Theresa's is that of workers divided – by skill, age, nationality, and by management. The nature of the catering operation accentuated divisions by allowing unequal treatment and unequal rewards. In a period of increasing unemployment, management successfully exploited these divisions in implementing their rationalization plan, which further fragmented the opposition and undermined militance. Absenteeism and bitterness were the price they had to pay for their success. Keeping the lid on these discontents was now their full-time occupation.

CHAPTER 2
The cooking factory

> This is not a kitchen, it is a production line, but we don't get production money!
>
> Mrs Sheila Greenhalgh, 58, cook at Michael Lansby

Michael Lansby is a community centre in the outskirts of a large northern city. Founded in the early 1970s, it includes a comprehensive school, colleges of further and adult education, an old-age pensioners' centre and a youth club, a public library and a skills centre, as well as extensive recreational and sports facilities. The centre, named after the mayor who provided the inspiration and the funds, was one of the last projects to materialize out of the great welfare vision, a concrete expression of the caring society at a local level. People's work, leisure, education and recreation were to be planned and administered by an enlightened central authority. Things did not work according to plan and the community refused to embrace the centre, whose facilities were constantly vandalized and defaced. The early idealism turned into cynicism and one of the catering managers described his department as an oasis in the midst of a 'socialist dream gone sour'.

Catering at Michael Lansby is very much part of the central plan. One large kitchen is designed to produce meals for everybody in the centre. These meals are cooked and packaged, then frozen and stored in a central refrigerating unit. From there they are transported to several satellite areas, where they are 'regenerated' and served.

In contrast to the unplanned, home-cooking methods of Saint Theresa's, the cook-freeze kitchen of Michael Lansby represents everything modern in catering technology; over the years its

The cooking factory

prodigious productivity has turned it into something of a showpiece in modern catering. At the time of my visit the cook-freeze kitchen produced on average 2,500 meals per day, which, after being frozen, were supplied to two comprehensive school dining-rooms (400 meals daily), an old-age pensioners' luncheon club (70 meals) and a meals-on-wheels service (100 meals), one adult education and two further education canteens, four snack-bars, one staff-social dining-room and one reserved for special functions. In addition, it supplied meals to 6 schools outside the precinct. The catering department employed in all 70 staff, corresponding to 45 full-time jobs.

On paper, the efficiency of the cook-freeze kitchen is truly outstanding, with 20 women on a single 7-hour shift producing as many meals as the 35 kitchen staff at Saint Theresa's. What makes this even more remarkable is that only 2 of these women have any catering qualifications. But then cooking at Michael Lansby was hardly a craft occupation; Ann Reynolds had worked in the cook-freeze kitchen since its opening, 11 years earlier:

> It's just like a factory making radios. It *is* a factory. When we prepare the food, we don't think that someone is going to sit down and enjoy it. As long as it looks all right we are not making any effort to improve the quality. There is no variety . . . Everything by the book, always the same way.

Cooking at Michael Lansby is done on three long stainless steel surfaces, the lines. One line produces the main courses, one the desserts and one the vegetables. Two to 5 women work on each line, while 2 work permanently on 2 pie-blocks. At the end of each line there is a wind tunnel where the meals are frozen in trays on trolleys. They are packed in plastic film by two or three women before they are stored in a large freezer at the end of the kitchen.

If Saint Theresa's kitchen and cooking methods represented an enlargement of home-cooking, the cook-freeze kitchen is the application of factory production in catering. The product is simple and uniform, cooked in large quantities in distinct stages with each worker carrying out a different task. Although most of the women rotate around the three lines monthly, there is little variety from day to day. On a given day, the vegetable line may do nothing other than produce frozen chips, the main line may produce 1200 pork pies and 240 portions of liver casserole, and the sweet line several hundreds of corn-flake pies and a thousand or more bread rolls. The recipes are simple and precise, as the menus for the schoolmeals are determined by the local Education Committee. The quantities of the different ingredients are carefully weighed, as are the contents of the trays before they are frozen. Everything appears to be organized and controlled by an invisible hand, that of the planner.

With the importation of mass-production techniques from manufacturing to catering comes the dissolution of the cook's traditional craft and its replacement by a carefully planned technological outfit. This trend is usually associated with the ideas of Frederick 'Speedy' Taylor, the father of scientific management. Taylor insisted that increased efficiency in manufacturing can only be achieved by placing management on a proper scientific foundation. He advocated a separation of execution from conception, in which management plan, organize and control the work, while workers carry out simple, standardized tasks in return for financial incentives. Under Taylor's scientific management, the thinking behind production is done in the lay-out and planning departments, while the workers's jobs are emptied of all individuality and creativity.

Taylor's ideas found numerous applications in the developing manufacturing industries in the United States since the turn of the century and gradually filtered through the manufacturing industries of other countries. More recently, similar ideas have been extensively applied to office organization and the service industries. The cook-freeze kitchen at Michael Lansby with its fragmented and standardized tasks, its systematic aversion towards skill, and its labour-saving devices, offers a perfect opportunity to study the effects of modern thinking in catering management on the workers.

By contrast to the high-tech organization of the kitchen, most of the satellite areas, where the frozen meals are transported, regenerated and sold, resemble those usually found in most schools and colleges. At the time of my visit, however, several of the dining-areas were being modernized. Having fallen prey to 'vandals', the old comfortable chairs, armchairs and tables were being replaced by new vandal-proof, bright-coloured seating arrangements fixed to the ground. Management had made a conscious decision of 'going fast food', an indication of who sets the standards as well as the styles in mass-catering today. Management were also thinking of revising the menus to include burgers and of dressing up the catering assistants in fast-food fashion. New computerized tills had been introduced a few weeks earlier to keep track of the performance of different dining-areas (and of individual staff) and of the demand for particular products.

The catering department was run by a team of 3 managers in their late twenties and thirties, 2 of whom had started together six years earlier. Bill Good, the catering manager, was assisted by two women deputies, one in charge of the cook-freeze and one for the 'end areas' but the three worked together as a team. The managers also cooked for special functions, using a well-equipped special kitchen next to the functions dining-room rather than the main cook-freeze kitchen. There was 1 clerical worker, 1 storeman and 3 porters. The remaining staff were classified as general kitchen assistants and assistant cooks – the latter, in spite of their job titles, were supposed to have a supervisory function. These were all women recruited locally, many of whom had worked at the centre since its beginning. Staff turnover was negligible and the background of the staff was very homogeneous. Except for two Irish women, everyone working at Michael Lansby was British. In the last couple of years, a few younger women had been recruited from school but the majority were married, middle-aged women with children. The main attraction of their jobs were the school holidays and the hours of work, which allowed them to look after their children when they were at home.

All workers and managers at Michael Lansby were part of a closed-shop agreement and belonged to one of the great general unions. Seven years prior to my visit there had been the first of two industrial disputes. A short wildcat strike had stopped management from putting catering staff in the old-age pensioners' dining-room on a 52-week work schedule (instead of the 40 weeks worked everywhere else on the site). A three-week strike a couple of years later had been less successful. It was sparked off by a demarcation incident involving one of the workers, but had turned into a dispute against a proposed reduction of work hours and, again, the abolition of 'school holidays' which went with the jobs. This had been necessitated by the reduction of the number of school-meals served but also by what management saw as over-manning and inefficiency. Yet, on the surface the strike was now forgotten and the proverbial 'new realism' had taken effect. Subsequent reductions in hours had not been resisted and new staff were not entitled to school holidays.

There was a cheerful atmosphere in most departments, with little of the tension which had been so obvious at Saint Theresa's. At lunch-time when the staff were having their free meal around four

The cooking factory

large tables much teasing, joking and chatting went on. On the first day of my visit the kitchen staff sang and gave a present to a disabled young woman who was leaving after having worked there as a trainee.

The field research

I spent one month at Michael Lansby, talking to workers and management informally and observing the way in which they worked. I also carried out structured interviews with 57 of the 70 working in the department. As at Saint Theresa's, it proved impossible to interview everyone due to limited time and staff illness, but there were no refusals.

TABLE 2.1
Distribution of sample at Michael Lansby by type of work

Position	Number in department	Number in sample
Management and clerical	5 (*)	5
Cook-freeze kitchen	20 (3)	17 (2)
Porters	3	3
Further Education and OAP dining-rooms	20 (3)	15 (3)
School-meals	12 (1)	8 (1)
Minor areas (**)	10 (1)	9 (1)
TOTAL	70 (8)	57 (7)

Note: Figures in parentheses are staff officially classified as assistant cooks, the remaining ones being classified as general kitchen assistants.

(*) includes the storeman
(**) includes snack-bar staff and staff working in smaller dining-rooms, in groups of less than 3

As can be seen from Table 2.2, 25 of the 52 workers had been in the department for 9 to 11 years, or virtually since the opening of the centre. The majority of the women were in their forties and fifties and only 7 were in their twenties (5 of them in the cook-freeze kitchen). Forty-two out of the 49 women workers were married; 40 of them had children of whom 29 had three or more. Most of them lived within walking distance or a short bus-ride away from work. Jobs at Michael Lansby attracted them because they could handle

61

TABLE 2.2
Length of service of sample at Michael Lansby

	M	CF	P	FE	SM	MA	D	All
Less than 2 years	0	2	2	2	1	1	4	8
2–5 years	1	7	1	5	1	1	7	16
5–9 years	4	0	0	1	1	2	4	8
9–11 years	0	8	0	7	5	5	17	25
TOTAL	5	17	3	15	8	9	32	57

M : Management and clerical
CF : Cook-freeze kitchen staff
P : Porters
FE : Further Education and OAP dining-room staff
SM : School-meals staff
MA : Minor areas staff
D : All dining-areas staff

them *within* their family lives. Several of them had left better-paid jobs for the holidays and the school-hours offered by their present jobs. Twenty of them had previously worked in factories and 8 in offices.

Job expectations and job satisfaction

The great importance the women attached to those work factors which did not interfere with their family lives is seen in Table 2.3. Hours, school holidays and convenient location were the commonest answers to the question 'What keeps you in this job?'

Like the ancillary workers at Saint Theresa's, most workers at Michael Lansby saw their work as 'just a job'. Their views, however, on what qualities a good job should have were very different. Interest and variety were seen as by far the most important features of a good job. After appropriate weighting for second and third choices, interest and variety obtained 21 per cent of all choices, followed by good workmates with 16 per cent and pay with 14 per cent. Among cook-freeze workers interest and variety obtained 24 per cent, good workmates 20 per cent and pay 18 per cent, with every other factor receiving less than 10 per cent.

Pay was important for virtually all groups of workers, but it was in every case topped by another factor, usually interest and variety and good workmates. Although pay was mentioned by 26 people as one of the three most important qualities of a good job, only 3

The cooking factory

TABLE 2.3
'What keeps you in this job?'

	M	CF	P	FE	SM	MA	All
'It's a job'/'The money'	1	13	3	9	5	2	33
Hours/school holidays	2	4	0	7	4	3	20
Convenient location	0	4	1	2	5	2	14
'I enjoy/like job/place'	3	3	0	2	0	5	13
'I like catering/cooking'	1	3	0	0	0	0	4
Workmates/friends/colleagues	1	1	0	1	3	1	7

Note. The figures in the above columns do not add up to the total number of staff in each category because several gave more than one reason.

M :Management and clerical
CF :Cook-freeze kitchen staff
P :Porters
FE :Further Education and OAP dining-room staff
SM :School-meals staff
MA :Minor areas staff

TABLE 2.4
Top four work priorities of staff at Michael Lansby

	M	CF	P	FE	SM	MA	D	All
Interest and variety	1	1	2	1	2=		2=	1
Pride in the product	2=	4=				3=		
Career in catering								
Helping others								
Good workmates		2		2=	2=	2	2=	2
Good working conditions				2=		1	1	4
Good supervision	2=	4=			1		4=	
Good pay and overtime	2=	3	3	4=	2=		4=	3
Job security				1	4=		3=	

M :Management and clerical
CF :Cook-freeze kitchen staff
P :Porters
FE :Further Education and OAP dining-room staff
SM :School-meals staff
MA :Minor areas staff
D :All dining-areas staff

1: Most frequently quoted quality of a desirable job; 2: Second most frequently quoted quality, etc.; =: equal placement

placed it top in their priorities. This suggests that the view of workers as 'instrumentally oriented' does not apply here; it is not true, in other words, that staff were prepared to do intrinsically

The cooking factory

unpleasant jobs because they regarded money as an adequate reward. Given the choice, most of the staff at Michael Lansby would like interesting jobs in the first place.

The 'craft' orientation of the cooks at Saint Theresa's was not so common at Michael Lansby. A majority did not particularly like cooking and only 2 saw working in catering or running a restaurant as their ideal job. Forty-one out of 52 women said that they would move out of catering if an opportunity arose. By contrast the 3 managers expressed a great interest in cooking, enjoyed cooking for special functions and were by general agreement very competent cooks.

The cook-freeze kitchen

The kitchen at Michael Lansby is dominated by the three long stainless-steel surfaces where the cooking is done, 'the lines'. Each line has its own cooking devices distributed along the length. The vegetable line has a variety of vegetable peelers and shredders, two steamers and two boilers. The pastry and sweet line has a heavy pastry mixer and a couple of ovens, while the meat line has two in-built vessels where stews are prepared, a variety of pie-blocks, a meat mincer and two more ovens.

Even at the height of activity, with 15 women working up and down the lines, everything looks remarkably clean and tidy. There are virtually no saucepans and pots, no accumulated washing-up, no dirty trays and cooking utensils. The floor is usually spotless. A radio is blaring well above its intended maximum volume. The women work quickly and efficiently, preparing the food, cooking it, packing it in re-cyclable plastic containers and, after it has cooled, placing it on trolleys in the three wind tunnels where it is frozen within a few hours.

At the other end of the kitchen, behind a glass partition, there is an office for the managers and the single clerical worker. Every four weeks they prepare a production sheet (they do not use the word 'menu') from a standard list of items, which, after being rubber-stamped by the council's catering officer, sets the targets of each line. This is the production sheet for the meat line on a typical week:

Monday: Bread pizzas (48 trays, 8 portions each), cheese and

onion pie (20 individual ones), individual pizzas (20), sausage rolls (50 × 8);
Tuesday: Pork pies (146 × 8), liver casserole (30 × 8);
Wednesday: Cottage pie (60 × 8), sausage rolls (50 × 8), meat pies (60);
Thursday: Cheese whirls (50 × 8), Cornish pasties (60 × 8), lamb casserole (60 × 8);
Friday: Bread mixes for schools

Recipes come from recipe books provided by the council to ensure that the nutritional standards of the meals meet their requirements; for example, 8 lb of flour is the minimum amount of flour for 100 dinners. Cooking standards are hardly those of haute cuisine. On a particular day, minced meat for shepherd's pies is, according to the recipe, boiled without being browned and then thickened by adding flour dissolved in water; 'gravy colourant', salt, onions and soya additive are then added and the mixture is boiled for a further twenty minutes. It is then placed in trays and covered with mashed potato made from powder.

On the same day, 3 women on the sweet line are preparing over 100 trays of 'corn-flake pies'. The trays are lined with pastry which is covered with jam. They are then filled with a mixture of crushed corn-flakes, syrup and butter and baked in a medium oven. Five women on the vegetable line will spend the entire shift peeling, cutting and steaming carrots. The vegetable line is regarded by everyone as the most boring, 'you are sick of the sight of vegetables by the end of the shift'.

Even at the peak of activity the easy-going atmosphere is striking. The radio, the continuous voices of people talking or joking but rarely shouting contrasted sharply with the high pressure and high-tension atmosphere of Saint Theresa's. Managers were rarely involved in direct supervision and could only be seen at times in the office behind the glass partition.

This cheerful, almost relaxed atmosphere was hardly ever broken during the month I was at Michael Lansby. It took, however, only the first few interviews to dispel the original impression that the women were happy with their jobs. One of the first cooks I interviewed was Mrs Mary Price, mother of four, who had worked in the cook-freeze kitchen since it opened and would retire in a few years' time. She was much respected by the other women and felt that she could speak on their behalf:

The cooking factory

> The girls in the kitchen are not happy. They all do it because they need the money. When the jobs were plentiful, you never saw young girls in the kitchen. The jobs are not good. No one enjoys their work here, only the bosses.

The main causes of the women's discontent were boredom, bad pay and bad management. Most women used the word 'factory' to describe what was unpleasant about their job. Mrs Norma Collins had also worked at Michael Lansby since it opened, having worked for many years in the textile industry:

> This is not really catering, more like working in a factory. The product is irrelevant, it's not like cooking at home – you just have to do everything by the book, the same day in day out. There is much less variety now, we used to do more different dishes.

Vivien Morris, in her early thirties, had been a typist before marriage; both of her children were now at school and she had started working at Michael Lansby a month earlier;

> I just don't like it, it's boring and monotonous; it's like working in a factory. Only the sweet line brings out your own abilities.

And Irene Robinson, who, with Karen Townsend, spent her entire shift packing the frozen meals in plastic wrap:

TABLE 2.5
Evaluation of own job by staff at Michael Lansby

	M	CF	P	FE	SM	MA	D	All
First rate	0	0	0	0	0	1	1	1
Pretty good	4	4	1	7	4	5	16	25
So-so	1	8	1	6	4	3	13	23
Not too good	0	4	1	2	0	0	2	7
Very bad	0	1	0	0	0	0	0	1
TOTAL	5	17	3	15	8	9	32	57

M   : Management and clerical
CF : Cook-freeze kitchen staff
P   : Porters
FE : Further Education and OAP dining-room staff
SM : School-meals staff
MA : Minor areas staff
D   : All dining-areas staff

There is no variety in the job; I would fall asleep doing it, if Karen ever stopped talking.

These comments are quite representative; only 4 of the 17 cooks found their jobs 'pretty good' (see Table 2.5). Although nobody expressed the profound indignation and despair of some of the staff at Saint Theresa's, the overall picture was considerably bleaker. In fact, the cooks at Michael Lansby expressed the lowest overall job satisfaction of any group of workers in any establishment. Four of the 8 who saw their job as 'so-so' qualified their answer; Mary Price:

> For me the job is so-so; at my age [59] I couldn't hope for anything much better; but I wouldn't recommend it to my daughter – I would hope she got something better. . . .

TABLE 2.6
'The main problem with my job is . . .'

	CF	P	FE	SM	MA	D	All
The job itself/boredom	7	1	5	2	3	11	18
Management/supervision	5	0	6	2	0	8	13
Bad pay	2	1	1	0	1	2	5
None	3	1	2	4	5	11	15
Others	0	0	1	0	0	0	1
TOTAL	17	3	15	8	9	32	52

M :Management and clerical
CF :Cook-freeze kitchen staff
P :Porters
FE :Further Education and OAP dining-room staff
SM :School-meals staff
MA :Minor areas staff
D :All dining-areas staff

TABLE 2.7
How interesting were their own jobs

	M	CF	P	FE	SM	MA	All
Interesting all the time	1	0	0	0	0	2	3
Interesting most of the time	4	6	0	10	5	7	32
Mostly dull and monotonous	0	7	2	4	3	0	16
Very dull and monotonous	0	4	1	1	0	0	6
TOTAL	5	17	3	15	8	9	57

The cooking factory

TABLE 2.8
Average Job Index scores at Michael Lansby

Management and clerical:	19.8
Cook-freeze kitchen staff:	14.3
Porters:	14.0
FE and OAP dining-room staff:	13.1
School-meals staff:	14.2
Minor areas staff:	14.7

High score indicates high level of job autonomy (27 = max score).
Low score indicates low level of job autonomy (9 = min score).

Boredom was the major source of dissatisfaction among cook-freeze workers. The poor quality of the jobs themselves is reflected in the low Job Index scores, shown in Table 2.8. The cooks' average score is not only well below that of the cooks at Saint Theresa's (18.6) but lower than that of kitchen porters in that establishment (16.2). *Not one* of the 17 cooks said that she could try her own ideas on the job and *all but two* found the job too simple to bring out their best qualities. Nearly all found their jobs too fast and too repetitive and only a handful thought that there was room for short-cuts. One of the cooks was the only person on my survey to score a minimum possible score of 9 points on the Job Index.

At Michael Lansby, there were none of the subtle personal touches of Saint Theresa's home-cooking style of catering. Only 3 of the 17 cooks described their jobs as skilled. 'Anyone could learn to do my job in a week or two,' said Anna Simmonds, a cook who had previously worked in the cotton and tobacco industries. The advanced catering technologies employed in the cook-freeze kitchen robbed the work of its creative aspect, reducing the jobs to the execution of precise instructions.

Yet, none of the women felt that they were part of a high-tech outfit. They saw their work as factory work, to be sure, but they saw their factory as part of a low-tech, low-wages industry. The jobs seemed menial and uninteresting, not much better than housework:

> It's the same boring job as what you do at home, but at forty-six it is hard to find another. There is no challenge in it, no excitement, most of the time it's dead boring.

Few of the women regarded technology as the main enemy; all but 2 felt that they controlled the machines and most of them said that machines were their friends not their enemies. New machines that had been recently introduced, like a steamer, a pie-blocker and a pastry-cutter, met with almost universal approval because they made work less tiring. In fact some of the women complained that the machines were not good enough; Mary Price:

> The machines may look modern but they are very old-fashioned. Cutting cabbage takes ages as you can see and also preparing the chips. On a busy day I have to lift the pastry-mixer up to a thousand times, winding it up and down; that's a lot of lifting.

Far from blaming technology for the poor quality of their jobs, the cook-freeze cooks (along with most other workers at Michael Lansby) felt trapped in undesirable jobs by their family obligations, their age and lack of qualifications and by the general economic climate. The majority felt tied to these jobs by their need for the money, which was important for making ends meet. Moira, mother of three at 30, had worked in an office before she got married; she had only been working at Michael Lansby for three years:

> My job is important for me, for the money and to get out of the home. At the moment, there are no other jobs I could do, with the children. But when they grow up I would like to get a more interesting job, textiles designing perhaps or clerical. I would like a job with responsibility, to feel that people depended on me.

And Vivien Morris:

> I would rather work part-time, that would be fairer to the family, wouldn't it. But we need the money, especially now that my husband has lost his job. This is why I am trying to make a go of it here.

The dining-areas

Unlike the cook-freeze staff, who worked 35 hours per week, most of the dining-room staff worked between 20 and 30 hours per week. Many of these women had had their hours cut by management by 3 or 4 hours per week in a savings drive. Two large Further Education cafeterias and the old age pensioners' dining-room adjoined the main kitchen and were frequently visited by management. Three groups of 6 to 7 women regenerated the frozen food in each of these three areas, served behind the counter and tidied up after mealtimes. They also did some cooking, ranging from beverages to snacks and light lunches, using relatively old-fashioned catering equipment.

These three large dining-areas, serving several hundreds of meals per day, were generally regarded as less desirable places to work than some of the more distant, smaller dining-areas and snack-bars. Most of them were run by women in twos or threes and were rarely visited by management, as some of them were in different buildings from the main kitchen. Two of the snack-bars had been refurbished in fast-food style and were extremely popular with the students and the public; one of them, a snack-bar immediately outside the public library, in which two women served only hot drinks, sandwiches and sweets, had a greater turn-over than the main dining-room for Further Education students. By contrast, the two dining-rooms reserved for teaching staff and special functions were mostly quiet and management had plans to change them.

The women working in these smaller dining-areas were by far the most satisfied in the entire department (see Tables 2.5, 2.6 and 2.7). Some of them were genuinely happy with their work. Margaret Platt and Rachel Bainbridge had worked together in a small snack-bar for over three years. The bar was several hundred yards away from the kitchen and the offices of management; it was a favourite meeting centre for groups of FE students who liked the comfortable armchairs and the busy, friendly atmosphere. This was Margaret's first job after marriage – she had previously worked in a mill:

> I like working in this small bar better than anywhere else; you get to know the students who come here, we have a laugh and a chat. The bosses leave us alone; it's a first-rate job.

Rachel had also worked in a factory, as well as in other dining-areas:

> I love my job; I like dealing with the youth of today. I am a mother figure to some of them. I was in hospital recently for an operation and they flooded me with cards and flowers. It's good to feel loved.

Only 2 out of 9 women working in these smaller areas said that their job was too simple to bring out their best qualities, compared to 17 of the 23 working in the larger areas. All 9 found their job interesting all or most of the time and only 2 said that their work was just another job.

While the catering assistants in the smaller areas found their jobs intrinsically satisfying, the majority of those working in the three large impersonal dining-rooms did not enjoy their jobs. Nine out of 15 women working there said that what kept them in their jobs was their need for the money. Yet, like the kitchen workers, most of these women thought that the main quality of a good job was interest and variety (see Table 2.4).

These two groups of women, the cooks and the assistants in the three large dining-rooms, knew each other well and spent their break and meal-times together. Their outlooks were quite similar in most respects. Cooking jobs were regarded as more monotonous and tiring, dining-room jobs were regarded as less safe and more likely to have their hours cut. Elaine Richards had originally worked in one of the smaller areas but had been moved to the Further Education dining-room recently:

> I asked to be moved because I was only working 12½ hours per week. I started here on 17 but already it has gone down to 15. Ideally I would like to work 25, but for the past few years there has been a constant loss of hours. The work is harder too, due to staff shortages.

However, the workers in these larger dining-rooms felt more job satisfaction than the cooks (although much less than the workers in the smaller areas). Seven out of 15 said that their job was pretty good. Compared with the cooks, they had a greater scope to influence their jobs. Many of them tried actively to introduce a personal touch to their work and make it more interesting. Pearl, one of the women working in a Further Education canteen, had won everybody's admiration by obtaining single-handedly management's permission to do some of 'her own cooking' in one of the areas. One of her workmates said:

> The food is great when she cooks; she makes curries and vegetarian dishes for Asian students. She even tries to improve the frozen stuff from cook-freeze to make it more tasty. She cares for her work and the students love her.

In contrast, then, to the regimented work routines of the cook-freeze kitchen, dining-room assistants enjoyed a certain degree of freedom at work which accounts for the fact that they found their jobs slightly more interesting and more satisfying.[1] The catering technology which they handled was relatively simple. However, a few weeks prior to my visit management had introduced computerized tills in the larger areas. The staff had initially been intimidated by them but by the time of my visit most of them said that 'they are easier to use, once you've picked up the way they work'. Five of the 10 women who used them, however, expressed reservations about the fact that the tills kept track of their performance:

> They are the Big Brother; they know how often you've served and they tell management how fast you've worked.

School-meals

The 10 women working in school-meals were all married with children. Most of them had been at Michael Lansby since its early days and they formed a strong and cohesive group. Together they had witnessed many changes. A few years before my visit the school-meals provision at Michael Lansby had 'gone cafeteria'; a cash-cafeteria counter service offering a choice of dishes replaced the traditional free meals consisting of meat and two vegetables. One immediate result of this change was that a larger number of children brought packed meals from home and the hours of the women working in the school dining-rooms had been cut. The dinner women worked an average of 25 hours, serving some 400 youngsters. All the food which they served originated in the cook-freeze kitchen.

At meal-times, the pressure was considerable, as children rushed from their classrooms to queue for their favourite dishes, which were not always in large supply. The atmosphere, however, was pleasant – the women knew the names of many of the children, they chatted with them as they served them, and kept the discipline in a firm but friendly manner.

Although the cafeteria system had lead to a reduction of their hours, it had generally improved the quality of their job; Sheila, with two of her three children at school in Michael Lansby, said:

> 'Going cafeteria' has been an improvement. Kids are happier now and they are easier to serve. My job is slightly more interesting now, and there is much less waste. There is more variety [in the job] now than before, when we had two set meals. But there is more rush now, as the kids rush to the

dining-rooms before we run out of the meals they like, pies, burgers, sausages; kids don't like fish in sauce and liver and they have less vegetables than they used to have.

Many of the women expressed reservations about the effect of the new system on the children's nutrition. Many of them disapproved of the food that some of the children were having:

> The kids who come late don't really have a proper dinner; some of them will just ask for a plate of chips or a pie.

> The meals would only provide good nutrition if the children got everything. But they usually choose pies and chips. What they get is fatty and stodgy.

Gill Moran, an outspoken, ebullient woman had won everybody's respect a few years earlier when she 'gave a piece of her mind' to the visiting council bureaucrats:

> It is easier for us now with the cafeteria system. But I don't like it; the first children to be served get the choice, the ones who come later don't have much choice and complain. There is a rush to be served early. We used to have a family service which was much better; now a lot of children have just a pie and chips and a cream-bun. We now serve a lot of junk food. It is easier to run the cafeteria style which we do now. Once the youngsters have eaten the [more popular] main course, the ones who come later end up eating just a plate of chips or a bar of chocolate. Pakistani children get no special dishes and end up having fish fingers every day. The bureaucrats from Prince Street who lay down all the regulations don't come here to see what the youngsters really eat.[2]

Like Gill, women in school-meals really cared about the quality of food which they served; they cared for the children and felt that they were doing something socially important. Their attitudes towards their job were generally positive, as shown in Tables 2.5 and 2.6. Although the job which they did was quite similar to that of the OAP and Further Education dining-assistants (in fact, there was more pressure in school-meals and less room for creativity), their devotion to the children gave meaning to their work; Sheila:

> The job can be monotonous. Sometimes I think that I was born

for something a bit better than this. But then I think of the kids and it all becomes worthwhile.

The strong altruistic orientation of these women is evident in the work they would choose to do in an 'ideal world'. Two of them would be nurses, 2 would run nurseries for children, 1 would take elderly people on foreign travel, 1 would be a missionary, 1 would be a personal secretary and 1 would look after her family at home. This orientation of school-meals women, their sense of doing something socially useful, their devotion to the children and their strong sense of solidarity, gave meaning to what would otherwise have been quite mundane jobs. But what tied them to these jobs was, as with most other groups, their need for the money.[3] Sheila:

> I enjoy the company of the other girls, I like the contact with the youngsters, but in the end it's the money that keeps me here; if I didn't need the money I would like something with more responsibility, doing voluntary work or going into nursing.

None of the 8 women I interviewed said that they enjoyed the job in its own right (see Table 2.3) and all 8 said that they would leave Michael Lansby if a better job came up elsewhere. Elaine Richards, a mother of four, like Sheila, had some reservations about the quality of their jobs:

> Monotony is the big drawback of this job. We have a rota moving from job to job, from the dishwasher to the counter, from the counter to the sink, but they are all the same. The job would be more satisfying if we did the cooking rather than just the regen. The cook-freeze problem is the opposite: they never see the people who eat the food.

To summarize: cooks in the cook-freeze kitchen found their jobs intrinsically boring, lacking in creativity and skill, but enjoyed better job security than the other groups. The assistants in the larger dining-areas also expressed considerable dissatisfaction with their work, but had greater scope to influence what they did and to introduce personal touches in their work. The women working in school-meals had very limited freedom in their work and their jobs were largely routine and boring; however, their strong altruistic orientation and their devotion to the children gave meaning to their work and raised their job satisfaction above that of the previous two groups. Finally, the assistants in the smaller areas, working in small groups of two or three, geographically scattered beyond the reach of the managers, expressed a high degree of job satisfaction, being able to socialize freely and informally with the customers and being free of direct supervision. They were the only group of workers who did not feel tied down to their jobs by financial need but actually enjoyed their work.

Wages

> I am not really dependent on my wage because I am lucky, my husband is working. My job is important for me all the same, it gives me a sense of independence.

Mrs Bainbridge, quoted here, was one of only 2 women whose wages were not necessary to help them make ends meet. For the remaining (including for those working very few hours), their wages were an essential part of the family budget. Seven of the 44 women who lived with their families were the only wage-earners of their household, their husbands being unemployed.

Yet, the women at Michael Lansby were even worse paid than the staff in Saint Theresa's. Women in the cook-freeze kitchen working a 35-hour week earned a basic £63 per week (£1.80 per hour), leaving them with £47 to £50 net after deductions. Staff working in the dining-areas were paid on hourly rates of between £1.70 and £1.75. These figures compare with average gross wages for all women working full-time in 1983 of £108.80 and for those in manual jobs of £87.90, and only 12.5 per cent of all full-time women and 25.1 per cent of those in manual jobs earned less than £1.80 per hour.[4]

Like the catering assistants at Saint Theresa's, all workers at Michael Lansby were among the 12 per cent worst-paid female workers and the 25 per cent worst-paid manual female workers. Yet, in spite of their low pay, pay only ranked third (after the jobs themselves and management) as a cause of dissatisfaction. As shown in Table 2.6, only 4 women (and 1 porter) in the total sample saw pay as *the main* problem with their work, compared with 18 who saw the job itself and 13 who saw management and supervision as the main problems.

Of course, there were some complaints, but then bad pay was

The cooking factory

usually seen as compounding a bad job. Karen Townsend, a young cook who had been at Michael Lansby for 3 years after a six-month stint on a Youth Opportunity Programme training scheme, lived at home with her parents. She said:

> The pay is absolutely lousy; the job is boring; I don't want to be here much longer. I am very musical and would like to do a better job or at least a better paid job with better working conditions.

Karen's expectations had not yet been lowered; most of the other women, however, seemed to accept their low wages as a reflection of a woman's limited market power. Gill Moran, the outspoken woman in school-meals, who had been a filing clerk at a solicitor's and then a nurse for 7 years, until an injury forced her to retire from the NHS:

> Of course, we are getting a pittance. But these are women's jobs, and women's jobs don't pay; nursing is a woman's job and it doesn't pay, most clerical jobs are women's jobs and they don't pay. Working in shops and supermarkets, cleaning offices, these are all women's jobs and they don't pay. You end up by accepting this; what you cannot accept is bad manners from the bosses.

Gill's views are quite representative. While the women at Michael Lansby had come to terms with their low wages as unavoidable in the present economic context, they found it much harder to come to terms with the other discontents.

Management at Michael Lansby

Next to the boredom and monotony of the work, the most important source of discontent was management. To begin with, I was surprised by this disaffection, for nobody could accuse management of being bossy or dictatorial. In comparison with some of the managers at Saint Theresa's, the 3 managers here seemed to be flexible and accommodating. Bill Good and Stella Bliss, the manager and deputy manager, were in their early thirties and had started work on the same day seven years earlier. They had been joined four years later by Victoria Cahill, a woman in her mid-twenties, who was in charge of the dining-areas, while Stella was in direct charge of the cook-freeze kitchen.

The 3 of them worked as a very close team and spent much time together. Unlike the managers at Saint Theresa's, they were not constantly pressed for time; 2 of the 3 were on day-release training courses. By their own account, less than a fifth of their time was spent on routine supervision and trouble-shooting. There were days when the cook-freeze kitchen functioned without a manager in sight until the end of the shift. Managers were rarely seen in the school dining-rooms or some of the distant satellite areas. 'We rely on the supervisors for the day-to-day supervision,' said one of the managers. By contrast the managers spent more time on cooking for special functions, on planning for the future, on the telephone, and on book-keeping and paperwork, which Bill Good described as the 'bane of his life' which absorbed more than a third of his working time.

Finally, the managers spent about another third of their time on what they generally referred to as 'staff'. Bill (he insisted on first names with me) was a self-made man, trained in both catering and management. Human relations were very important to him and his relaxed almost casual manner could not make a sharper contrast to the highly controlled manner of Mr Sprake at Saint Theresa's.

> I regard management as getting things done through people. My biggest source of concern is 'staff'. You become a social worker among other things in this job. In everything you do, you must constantly show regard for people's feelings. Staff problems today are not the same as when we took over, in that they don't threaten the operation – but they take a lot of my time to sort them out. They are awkward demands which have to be dealt with, a dinner lady who wants a day off, a cook who wants to move to another section, that sort of thing.

Bill's account of the problems of industrial relations which he had inherited is diplomatically phrased but leaves no ambiguity about his determination to use his power, and his pride in having done so.

> When Stella and I first came here in 1977, the union was very aggressive and so was the catering manager. The sparks flew. His predecessor had wanted to be just a figurehead; the union saw his weakness and tried to exploit it. There was a wildcat

> strike because he decided without consultation that the staff should work 52 weeks per year [instead of the normal 40 with paid school holidays]. When we took over we had a bit of a showdown with staff. We took disciplinary action against a lady who refused to work in a different job [a demarcation problem] and they went out on strike. We had also had to reduce their hours of work, as a result of the drop in the number of school-meals. Nobody wins such situations, but they were let down by their union, I must say, and they came back to work on our terms, three weeks later. This was the big storm which cleared up the air; they now accept what we say. They are very co-operative. But you have to treat them with respect. . . . Now we all know where we stand; a new realism has descended on the workers, who accept that the hours have to be cut down and that staffing levels must be cut.

Like the managers at Saint Theresa's, Bill Good saw the workers' co-operativeness as stemming from their new realism. He had good reason to be satisfied with his workers. A new contract had been drawn up for new recruits without opposition, and the new staff were not entitled to paid school holidays. Nor had staffing reductions of about 25 per cent (through 'natural wastage') been resisted. The weekly hours (excepting those in the kitchen) had been reduced by an average of 2, with no organized resistance. During my visit, a local election was held on the Michael Lansby site and staff from school-meals were re-deployed in the cook-freeze kitchen, with no apparent resentment.

What were the workers' attitudes towards their bosses? The commonest answer to my question of whether management was doing a good job running the department was 'The bosses are not running this department, the girls are.' Norma Collins had worked in the cook-freeze kitchen since the opening:

> Mrs Bliss doesn't have a clue of what is going on in the kitchen. As long as the work gets done she just stays out of it. Just as well, mind you!

And Mary Price:

> The bosses spend very little time in the kitchen as you can see yourself; they really don't understand many of our problems, like working with faulty equipment. . . . They don't run the department, the girls do.

TABLE 2.9
Staff attitudes towards management

	CF	P	FE	SM	MA	D	All
My manager is:							
friendly and informal	4	0	2	5	6	13	17
formal and impersonal	9	3	7	1	1	9	21
correct but unfriendly	3	0	5	2	2	9	12
pushy and bossy	1	0	1	0	0	1	2
TOTAL	17	3	15	8	9	32	52
Management is doing							
a good job	3	1	0	3	2	5	9
a good job for themselves but bad for the staff	3	0	5	1	1	7	10
a bad job	10	2	9	3	3	15	27
don't know	1	0	1	1	3	5	6
TOTAL	17	3	15	8	9	32	52
Managers are arrogant to their staff							
disagree	2	2	2	3	2	7	11
agree	13	1	13	4	5	22	36
don't know	2	0	0	1	2	3	5
TOTAL	17	3	15	8	9	32	52

CF : Cook-freeze kitchen staff
P   : Porters
FE : Further Education and OAP dining-room staff
SM : School-meals staff
MA : Minor areas staff
D   : All dining-room staff

The style of management of the bosses at Michael Lansby can best perhaps be described as 'laissez-faire' – as long as the kitchen and the dining-rooms operated smoothly (which was most of the time) management were content to take a back-seat. In order to understand this style of management it is important to look at the function of management at Michael Lansby. This function was shaped by the cook-freeze technology which dominated the catering operation at the centre, the technology which seeks to minimize the human factor by the standardization and fragmentation of production and the separation of the conception from the execution. Burawoy (1985:40ff) argued that such techniques have transformed the problem of moral legitimacy of management into a technical

The cooking factory

problem of production efficiency. The true triumph of Taylorism, he argues, is not as a theory or a practice for managers but as an ideology of management legitimacy. The right to manage lies in the fact that in modern industry managers are *technically indispensable*. As the worker is reduced to a cog on the machine, managers are indispensable for planning, co-ordinating and trouble-shooting. So long as work was done by craftsmen who knew their trade, managers could only be seen as oppressors and exploiters. Once work has been reduced to the passive acting out of routines, management becomes technically indispensable. Just try to imagine a car assembly line which operates without the massive managerial support.

It is very interesting then that most of the cooks at Michael Lansby felt that management was redundant. Bernadette, one of only 2 cooks with catering qualifications and in charge of one of the three lines:

> The bosses here keep themselves to themselves and are very arrogant with us. As long as the work gets done they don't care about you. Mrs Bliss just doesn't notice what is going on in the kitchen. Today, for instance, there were only three girls on the meat line and she didn't take much notice. I had to get Marie from the veg line to come and help us. Most of the time the girls run the department.

Cook-freeze technology, the technology of catering mass production, far from legitimizing management control seemed to make it redundant. It is true that 'management' or 'the faceless bureaucrats of Prince Street' had planned the department, had purchased the machinery, had determined the products and every aspect of how it should be prepared. Having done all this, however, control became assimilated in the process itself, leaving no actual function for the managers. While Taylorism may have bolstered the legitimacy of management as a function, in a contradictory way, it undermined the power of the actual managers. Unlike the managers at Saint Theresa's who had and exercised considerable amounts of power, all 3 managers at Michael Lansby complained that they didn't have enough power. Bill Good:

> There is little room for initiative; initiative is not rewarded by Prince Street [council headquarters]. I wish we had a more enlightened system. We just have to follow the directives of

faceless bureaucrats. This causes us considerable aggravation. There are few decisions which we can make without their approval.

Some of the workers had realized the relative impotence of their managers in their relations with the council headquarters. Mrs Anna Simmonds:

> You ought to be here when Miss McDermott [the council's catering officer] is expected on a visit. The bosses run around like mad all day making sure that the place is spotless, last time they even threw the mops away in their panic, they didn't have time to put them away. . . . They never dare open their mouth, it's Gill from school-meals who does all the talking.

Irene Robinson made a similar point about the managers' difficulties in dealing with staff problems:

> They just can't make a decision. They don't take responsibility. I've never known bosses like this, who can't make a decision. They will never say 'no' to you but they will never say 'yes' either.

Andre Gorz has provided the following explanation for the powerlessness of both managers and workers in modern industry:

> The great secret of large-scale industry . . . is that *nobody holds power*. Power in such organisms does not have a subject; it is not the property of individuals freely defining the rules and goals of their collective actions. Instead, all that can be found – from the bottom right up to the top of an industrial or administrative hierarchy – are agents obeying the categorical imperatives and inertias of the material system they serve. (1982:52)

If managers at Michael Lansby had little autonomous power it was because they did not require it in order to ensure control within their organization. In contrast to the 'simple control' exercised by the managers at Saint Theresa's, who relied on continuous supervision and the arbitrary application of sanctions and rewards to ensure discipline, control at Michael Lansby was what Edwards has termed 'technical'. It was assimilated in the production process itself and managers rarely had to rely on arbitrary exercise of power.

Given the absence of supervision why did things run so smoothly? I asked Mary Price, one of the older cooks:

> Of course we always meet the quotas. The bosses can never find something to blame in our work; things never go missing, the standards are kept up, we always meet the targets for the day, the place is clean. That's how we keep the bosses off our backs most of the time.

This is a point of great importance. By meeting the production sheets and working harmoniously together, the women kept the bosses out of the kitchen. Far from being pawns in the bosses' games, the women's acceptance of the rules of the game gave them relative freedom from direct supervision. This is a highly valued freedom, the freedom to talk about what they liked, to laugh at what and at whom they liked, without being watched. The kitchen was their space, where managers had to tread with circumspection, preferring to stay behind the glass partition or in their own offices for as long as things worked smoothly.

By submitting themselves to what Edwards calls 'technical control', the women in the cook-freeze kitchen established some control over their work environment and even over their work. They could adjust the pace of work so that miraculously the job for the day was always completed by a quarter to four, they could divide the work evenly among themselves or rotate individual tasks. Self-management was in this way a step towards regaining a measure of control in their own job; this did not make boring jobs enjoyable, but it made them bearable.

Management laissez-faire at Michael Lansby, then, was, in my view, the outcome of a compromise in which the workers were, in effect, saying 'Stay out of our way and we will deliver the goods.' This compromise, however, did not bridge the divide between the two sides. In fact, although workers at Michael Lansby enjoyed the laissez-faire, they found their managers more objectionable than the staff at Saint Theresa's found their firm and authoritarian one. Only 9 out of 52 thought that management did a good job, in contrast to 27 out of 53 at the hospital. There were three main and inter-related criticisms of management. First, that their manners were arrogant (36 out of 52), second, that they didn't care for their staff (37 out of 52) and third that there was no consultation between workers and management (all 52).

The first criticism surprised me, in the face of Bill's strong views on human relations. Most of the workers either did not notice the management's attempt at human relations or regarded it merely as

The cooking factory

a façade. As is shown in Table 2.9, two-thirds of them regarded the bosses as formal and unfriendly as well as arrogant at times. Irene Robinson:

> They're dead formal and impersonal. I am older than them and still they call me with my first name but they insist on being called Mr and Mrs.

Criticisms of arrogance blend with the other two criticisms; Marie Purvis, one of the school-meals assistants:

> They could do a better job. They are inconsiderate at times; because they see you in an overall they think that you've got no brains at all. You see things that they don't. They don't explain things to the girls, for example what is happening with the new school [for which the cook-freeze kitchen was about to start cooking].

Gladys, a dining-room assistant:

> They are *very* arrogant. They never show appreciation or gratitude to the girls. They don't believe you when you are ill. They don't try to make life easier for the girls. . . . They don't communicate enough with their staff, they are not interested in you (as a person) – they are only concerned with you doing the work.

Some of the women tried to give managers the benefit of the doubt. Mrs Maureen Byers, another of the cooks who had worked since the opening of Michael Lansby, after earlier jobs in the cotton and tobacco industries:

> She [Mrs Bliss] tries but can't really understand. If you don't have children you cannot understand how people with children feel.

Moira, a dining-room assistant:

> Some of the managers are too young and not considerate. Some have better manners, not that it gets you anywhere talking to them. There is no consultation between them and us. They just plonked the new tills here, talked to us just for ten minutes about it.

A climate of mistrust prevailed, with the workers feeling that their lives were likely to be affected crucially by decisions made

The cooking factory

behind their backs, decisions over which they had no influence and which were only going to be communicated to them as faits accomplis. Sheila Greenhalgh:

> You are the last one to learn when they change something; and even then you learn from the grapevine; they do not consult with us.

This led to a constant sense of insecurity and fear. *Not one* of the 52 workers felt that there was adequate consultation with management and only a few thought that there was adequate communication.

While, in their discussions with me, no manager showed lack of consideration for their staff, their attitude towards consultation was negative; one of the assistant managers:

> In a field like catering you cannot involve them in decision-making; they wouldn't know what we are talking about. They lack the skills and the ability.

What is ironic is that the Michael Lansby managers were themselves victims of the same dismissive attitude from headquarters; they themselves complained about the lack of consultation with their superiors and about being presented with faits accomplis. Although the managers resented the pressures applied by those above them they did not seek to bridge the gap between them and their subordinates.

> There is aggravation whenever things go wrong; but most of the time when things go right you get no praise at all.

This complaint, coming from one of the managers, simply echoed the views of many of her subordinates towards her.

Unions

The women's complaints against the managers' arrogance were compounded by the feeling that they were entirely ignored by the union. They all belonged to one of the general unions as part of a closed-shop agreement, which covered all ancillary workers on the Michael Lansby precinct. Managers were not covered by the closed-shop agreement, but all 3 catering managers had chosen to join the management section of the same union.

Catering workers felt with considerable justification that the union was merely interested in checking-off their dues. Since the defeat of the strike several years earlier (when, according to Bill Good, they had been let down), the union had taken little interest in the catering workers' work and conditions and had made no active attempt to organize them. The union official was only seen once or twice per year, and several of the cooks said that 'he is more friendly with the bosses than with us'. This view was backed by a manager who confided in me that the union man gave warning 'if trouble is brewing'.

Several of the workers were bitter about the union. Sheila Greenhalgh:

> Of course I am a committed unionist. I believe in what the unions stand for. But in this place, the same union represents both management and workers; its representative spends more time with the bosses than with us. What good can come of it?

And Susana Walby, a dining-room supervisor, who had also been at Michael Lansby since its opening:

> I don't believe in all that unions do, but in most of it. They haven't done much for their members here, have they? We went on strike, all for nothing – we were fighting to protect our holidays, you see, to stop management cutting our hours too. But the union did nothing for us.

Both the closed-shop and the check-off system operated at Michael Lansby to muffle and incorporate unionism, in a way which echoes the observations of Nichols and Beynon in a chemical plant (1977:108ff) and Anna Pollert in a tobacco factory (1981:159). In catering, however, exclusion from collective bargaining and the lack of union support over grievances were perceived as part of the second-class citizenship of all catering workers. Mary Price:

> Working in catering you feel sometimes that your job lacks dignity. Kitchen ladies and catering staff generally are treated as inferior people by everyone. The unions don't do enough to improve our conditions or status. Within the union we are second-class citizens.

This view of catering staff as inferior people was one which I encountered in *every* catering establishment I visited. The issue of *dignity* in catering is extremely important. It appears that, apart

TABLE 2.10
Attitudes towards unions

	CF	P	FE	SM	MA	D	All
'I have only joined the union because of the closed shop'							
Agree:	1	0	5	2	2	9	10
Disagree:	16	3	10	6	7	23	42
TOTAL	17	3	15	8	9	32	52
'Would you describe yourself as a committed trade unionist?'							
Yes:	11	0	3	3	3	9	20
No:	5	1	10	4	5	19	25
Don't know:	1	2	2	1	1	4	7
TOTAL	17	3	15	8	9	32	52
'We need union protection'							
Agree:	16	2	15	7	8	30	48
Disagree:	1	1	0	1	1	2	4
TOTAL	17	3	15	8	9	32	52
'We need union help over pay and conditions of work'							
Agree:	15	3	14	7	7	28	46
Disagree:	0	0	1	1	2	4	4
Don't know	2	0	0	0	0	0	2
TOTAL	17	3	15	8	9	32	52

CF : Cook-freeze kitchen staff
P : Porters
FE : Further Education and OAP dining-room staff
SM : School-meals staff
MA : Minor areas staff
D : All dining-room staff

from all the other grievances of catering workers (working conditions, low pay, bad hours etc.), low status is widely felt in all but the most glamourous sectors of their trade.[5] It is a grievance that unites workers *and management* in catering. Miss Cahill, one of the assistant managers:

> In catering you are always looked down on by people. In this place, teachers think that they are better than us, status-wise.

The low status of their jobs was, in the workers' view, compounded by two facts – that they were women and that many of them worked part-time. Liz, a dining-room assistant:

Because we are part-time and all women they don't take us seriously. They don't come to talk to us and we never seem to get anywhere with them. They never follow up our suggestions; they say 'We'll see what we can do' when problems arise but never do anything.

In spite of the total dissatisfaction and disillusionment with the union, only 10 of the workers said that they would opt out of the union if there was no closed-shop and none of them expressed grave concern or unhappiness about the arrangement. On the contrary, the overwhelming majority thought that they needed both union protection and union help over pay and working conditions, as is shown in Table 2.10.

What is perhaps more surprising is that the majority of the full-time employees and a significant minority of the part-time ones saw themselves as committed union members and would welcome greater involvement in union matters. Such views clearly contradict traditional attitudes of women towards unions like the ones described by Anna Pollert:

> Most women were not ashamed to admit their ignorance about unionism. The language was alien, and merely confirmed their sense of exclusion from this 'man's world'. In fact, their exclusion confirmed their belonging to the other, 'women's world', and also reinforced their sense of femininity. (1981:159f)

Unlike Pollert's respondents but like the catering assistants at Saint Theresa's, most of the women at Michael Lansby were neither ignorant of unions and unionism nor (as they had proven on two earlier occasions) unwilling to use militant collective action to protect their jobs, their holidays and their hours. However, their experience with their union when they needed it in pursuit of *their* interests, i.e. holidays and hours, had taught them that they could not rely on the men's support.

Cook-freeze technology and alienation

The catering department at Michael Lansby represented an uncomfortable compromise of tradition and automation in catering. The cook-freeze kitchen was a faithful adoption of Taylorist principles in mass catering, splitting-up cooking from planning, breaking up work-tasks into simple and tightly controlled routines, and reducing the skill, initiative and thinking required of the cooks to a virtual minimum. Labour-saving catering technology is introduced on a massive scale, transforming 'cooks into unskilled materials handlers'. (Rothschild, 1981:16) The kitchen itself becomes a factory, mass-producing food, as many of my respondents were quick to point out. All freedom and creativity, the hallmarks of craft cooking, are eliminated through rules aimed at preventing the cooks from 'messing about with the recipes'. Monotony and lack of variety prevailed, each day being the same as the previous one.

Most of the dining-areas, on the other hand, were at the time of my visit organized along traditional lines. However, two areas had already been re-styled as fast-food restaurants and there were plans to do so in others. While this was primarily aimed at combating vandalism, management was clear about its other advantages – greater turn-over of customers, less cleaning and tidying, neater, simpler tasks. Plans of further rationalization of eating areas existed, but at the time of my visit they had not yet been implemented.

In contrast to the prodigious productivity of the cook-freeze kitchen (about 100 meals per shift per person) that of the serving areas was not unlike the productivity of ordinary canteens. The part-time staff of these areas were more satisfied with their jobs and they found their jobs more interesting than the cook-freeze staff. Staff working in the smaller snack-bars and dining-rooms, rarely visited by management, expressed considerable satisfaction with their jobs; by common consent, however, they were the ones whose jobs were most at risk.

The cheerful efficiency which prevailed in the kitchen and the esprit de corps among the women had not prepared me for the degree of dissatisfaction expressed by the cook-freeze staff. Their main complaints were boredom at work and management behaviour. This may be seen as confirmation of Braverman's and Blauner's views that mass production deskills the jobs and alienates the workers, but certain qualifications are necessary. While it is true that *as a group* cook-freeze staff found their jobs boring and unsatisfying, the ones who were most unsatisfied were not the ones who found their jobs least interesting; nor were they the ones who found their jobs most restricting, according to the Job Index. It was in fact the women whose job expectations were primarily for interest and variety who found their jobs most dissatisfying.

Nor did the high-tech work environment prevent the workers from establishing group bonds and cause isolation, as Blauner's work might have suggested. Twelve of the 17 cooks said that they talked 'a good deal' during work and as I was able to observe all of the talking and joking was about things outside work, personal appearance, kids, husbands, TV programmes and so on. In spite of its great influence on the nature of the women's work, technology should not therefore be seen as having the final say on every aspect of their work behaviour.

Moreover, the cooks' experience at Michael Lansby suggests that even where scientific management and deskilling technology deprives the workers of active control, pockets of resistance exist, areas in which the workers seeks to use their initiative, express their own creativity and establish some measure of control. Earlier I gave the example of Pearl, the dining-room supervisor who had of her own initiative started cooking curries and vegetarian dishes, in addition to the regenerated meals. These improvised meals which had proved most successful showed that she loved cooking, took great pride in what she prepared and tried to find some 'space' within which she could use her own judgment and skill. This was just one instance where against all odds an individual used her own ability and skill to create a little sphere of self-expression and control at work.

Workers in the cook-freeze kitchen had less opportunities of asserting a similar type of control over their work. Even there, however, women could control the pace of their work and, within the groups working on each one of the three lines, they could assign the work among themselves without management interference. By meeting the production targets and by showing that they could manage themselves, they kept management interference low and turned the kitchen into their place, where they could talk and laugh free of supervision. Some of the older ones did not much care for the radio blaring continuously in the kitchen – they all saw it, however, as their own stamp on their work environment, which no amount of management planning could eliminate.

These small areas of control made their work bearable. They also enhanced their solidarity, grown out of shared interests and common home backgrounds, and promoted through constant chatting. No other group in this study displayed the same feeling of togetherness, the same devotion to each other and the same uniformity of outlook as the women at Michael Lansby. This feeling of togetherness provided consolation for jobs devoid of interest. Fourteen out of the 17 women working in the kitchen said that they had made friends at the workplace and 12 of them met with their friends outside work. All 32 dining-assistants had made friends and about half met their friends outside the workplace. Thirteen of them said they would be very upset and another 14 fairly upset if they had to move away from their workmates.

All but one women in the entire sample felt that teamwork and co-operation was good, even though for some it was no compensation for the monotony of the job. Moira who worked in the Further Education dining-room:

> Teamwork is good; we all get on together very well. We help each other a lot. But we are all basically dying to get through the day.

And Mrs Sheila Greenhalgh, from the cook-freeze kitchen:

> It's a good job that we get on together because the job itself is not much good. . . . The girls here must have a sense of humour in order to cope.

As Paul Willis has argued, 'having a laugh' is one of the earliest ways working-class children pick up as a way 'to defeat boredom and fear, to overcome hardship and problems – as a way out of almost everything' (1978:29). 'Having a laugh' through jokes and caricatures has also been a major political gesture, through which the weak get their own back on those in authority. Humour turns a painful experience into an occasion for emotional discharge and even celebration.

For the women at Michael Lansby, especially those working in the cook-freeze kitchen, humour was a major survival technique, building up solidarity and relieving the discontents of work. Unlike at Saint Theresa's, these discontents did not manifest themselves as staff turnover and absenteeism. Nor were they channelled into organized union activity, from which the women were all but excluded. Nor did they take the form of 'sabotage', withdrawal of good-will or shoddy work; on the contrary, the staff were repeatedly described to me by managers as hard-working and co-operative. It seems then that the women were able to live with their jobs, rely on each other's support, enjoy each other's company, have a laugh together and for the time being make the best of it.

Like the workers at Saint Theresa's, the majority of the workers at Michael Lansby felt trapped in their jobs. Like the workers at Saint Theresa's, they found age and the general economic situation were major obstacles to changing jobs. But while for the first group their language difficulties, lack of skills and fear of the unknown contributed to the feeling of being trapped in their jobs, the women at Michael Lansby were tied to their jobs due to their 'family obligations'. Maureen Byers and Jean Harrison had both worked at Michael Lansby since its opening; they were both in their fifties, Jean with two of her six children living at home, Maureen with all four. They both had to shop, cook, wash, clean and tidy at home, in addition to working 9 to 4 in the cook-freeze kitchen. Jean:

> The only thing that keeps me here is the money. At my age it's not so easy to find another job with [school] holidays and suitable hours. It's not worth leaving now. I'd like to leave though, because you're treated like children.

Maureen:

> I couldn't get school holidays and hours like these anywhere else. How could I look after my family, where would I find the time?

The traditional position of women at home, the need to look after children and cook for husbands and the endless burden of housework tied them to their jobs. Only 4 out of 42 women living with their husbands said that their husbands helped with the cooking and only 5 got any help in shopping. Many of them looked after two, three or four school-age children. Their lives outside the workplace was hardly spent on what sociologists like to call leisure activities. Sarah, a dining-room assistant:

> You cook, you serve, you wash up, you clean, you tidy up. You go home, and you do the same things, you cook, you serve, you wash up, you clean, you tidy up.

School holidays and suitable hours were the main asset of their job, not because they afforded them leisure time but because they were compatible with their second job – their work at home. It is also what tied them to their work. It is not accidental that the threat to their holiday entitlement was one of the factors which brought them out on strike. Living in 'a man's world' placed additional burdens on some of them. One of the dining-assistants:

> I'd love to do something more interesting, not really in catering,

perhaps being a rep or clerical, something not quite as repetitive. I trained as a hairdresser but my husband, you see, is very jealous and doesn't let me work in hairdressing. This, he thinks, is all right, a woman's job.

Living with a bad deal described the feelings of many of the workers at Michael Lansby. However, when asked what they would like to do in an ideal world, a torrent of frustrated dreams surfaced. Some said that they would like to 'work at home' but many said that they wished they could do something different which would give them real satisfaction, like being a politician, a nanny, a nurse, an air-hostess, a telephonist, a musician, a social worker. Like Huw Beynon's respondents at Fords, many expressed a wish to do a 'worthwhile' job or a 'responsible' job:

> My ideal job, what I'd like to do in an ideal world would be to do voluntary work in a hospital, with children. Making them feel happy. It would give me a real sense of satisfaction and achievement.

> I would like to do mission work, not from a religious point of view, you see, but something with a sense of purpose in it. Like working in a hospital curing and healing people, bringing the smile back to their faces.

> I would like to travel, to take disabled people on holidays.

> You won't believe this. I'd like to be a boss; to achieve something, to be in control – just to see what it's like to be on the other side of the fence. I feel awful about confessing that.

These flights of fantasy, along with the oft-repeated dream of winning the pools, were all too clearly recognized as fantasies; they were seen as fantasies of escapes from lives which did not appear as a series of choices, but as sequences of inevitables, from home to work, to marriage, to children, to work; from home to work and from work back home.

CHAPTER 3
The fun food machine

> It's all artificial. Pretending to offer personal service with a smile when in reality no one means it. We know this, management know this, even the customers know this, but we keep pretending. All they want to do is take the customer's money as soon as possible. This is what it's all designed to achieve.
>
> Sheila, 19,
> a fast-food worker

Fast food did not get its name for nothing: speed is one of the secrets of its success. As the spearhead of the great 'refuelling revolution' in catering, the fast-food outlet is an assembly line which churns out a uniform and reliable product on a regular and repetitive basis. The hamburger, the industry's acclaimed Model T, is carefully planned to appeal to a world market. Vast technical and human resources (to say nothing of the animals) are involved in its production – cooking would be a word hopelessly misplaced in this context. As an executive acknowledged, the fast-food chain is 'not a chef system but a food management system';[1] or as Alison, a fast-food worker, said, 'this is not cooking, it is imitation cooking.'

Fast food does not merely represent the extreme application of highly sophisticated technologies in catering; it also represents an important social force which has moulded and transformed the eating habits of many people, earning for the youth of the 1970s the nickname of the 'hamburger generation'. The meal as social occasion is replaced by a type of eating on the move. Eating for enjoyment and pleasure is replaced by the quick consumption of a meal experience, food plus image, in short functional eating masquerading as fun eating. 'We'll help you make a meal of it,' proclaims an inadvertently candid fast-food advertisement.

The fun food machine

Based on the efficient production of a standardized product and its success in glamorizing it, the growth of fast food has been prodigious. In the United States, the number of jobs 'created' in fast food in the 1970s exceeded the total number of jobs in the steel and automobile industries combined. McDonald's, the fast-food world leaders, employ more people than the entire steel industry and, according to some estimates, over half their customers in the year 2000 will be former employees of the company.

Fast food is an international phenomenon. In November 1985 there were 8,600 McDonald's outlets worldwide. Kentucky Fried Chicken, a subsidiary of one of the world's largest companies, had over 7,000 outlets in 50 countries selling over 2.5 billion pieces of chicken annually – enough chickens to go around the earth six abreast when arranged head to tail. Several more fast-food chains have more than a thousand outlets each worldwide (including Wendy Hamburgers, Burger King and Pizza Hut), while the British-based Wimpy International has approximately 600 outlets in over 20 countries.

In the UK over 1000 hamburger, over 1350 pizza and over 650 chicken outlets have opened in the past fifteen or twenty years. In 1986 McDonald's had 200 outlets (up from 81 in 1982) and employed 15,000 people (up from 6,300 in 1982) of whom 75 per cent were under 21 years and the majority worked part-time. Kentucky Fried Chicken had over 360 stores, of which 300 were franchise operations, and predicted 'at least 150 new stores' in the next five years; its turnover in 1983 exceeded £75 million. Wimpy, Britain's traditional fast-food leaders with over 370 table-service franchises, joined the counter-service band-wagon and controlled 89 such outlets, double the number of two years earlier.

With three out of four workers in fast food under 21 and an annual staff turn-over estimated at 300 per cent (i.e. average stay with the company of about 4 months), it is not surprising that fast food is one of the few sectors which can still offer large numbers of jobs to school-leavers. Working in fast food is now the commonest choice as a first job in Britain. A stint at the fast-food outlet is part of the work experience of an increasing number of young people. Yet relatively little has been written about them. Studying fast-food workers at the place of work is extremely difficult. The secrecy which prevails reaches levels of institutional paranoia. In the crew handbook of one of the industry's leaders the following is given as an act of dishonesty and gross misconduct, leading to summary dismissal:

> Disclosing, or making statements, to any person, including press, radio, television and media representatives, any information relating to the Company, its business or affairs, its customers or finances, or any of its trade secrets at any time during the continuance of your employment.

After protracted negotiations with three firms, one of them agreed to offer me limited access to interview some of its staff and management in three of its London stores. Fun Food International is one of the giants of the fast-food trade; with several hundred stores in the United Kingdom, it figures prominently among the world's 25 largest catering companies.[2] The company owes its reputation to the hamburger, which remains its best-selling product, but is now also selling fish, chicken and a breakfast package. In addition to being one of the largest fast-food franchises in Europe, Fun Food also runs a substantial number of its own stores.

If the catering system at Michael Lansby combined a high-tech cooking operation with traditional cafeteria serving, Fun Food involves rationalization through and through. The products, the service, the cooking, the seating arrangements, the location of the stores, the technological hardware and software, are all determined according the principle that there is 'one best way'. The work itself, the storing and unpacking of materials, the cooking, wrapping and presenting of the products, the appearance of the staff and the way they address the customers, are all laid down to the smallest detail in rules and regulations.

Staff are constantly reminded that there is one best way of doing the job. The Training Department's instructions to the new employee states:

> WHAT IS IMPORTANT is that you should *understand* WHY YOUR work has to be done in a certain way and that you do it properly, to the best of your ability. NOT BECAUSE YOU HAVE TO, but because YOU WANT TO. In the end this is the BEST WAY.

And this is a message which is definitely accepted by a substantial number of staff. Mike, an 18-year-old worker who had only been with Fun Food for a fortnight, said:

There are no short-cuts in this job; they have perfected the best way of doing things and you have to stick to it. You just follow the rules.

While the execution of each task is strictly specified, the assignment of tasks is flexible, with supervisors and managers frequently serving behind the counter at peak times. Staff members are divided between 'production', counter-service and customer areas on an informal basis. Demarcation lines in fast food are blurred. This is the result of the central difference between an assembly line producing cars and one producing hamburgers. In the car line the speed of the line controls the speed of work.[3] In the fast-food production line the speed of the line must vary constantly depending on the numbers of customers – demand varies from moment to moment and quick redeployment of forces becomes essential.

The interdependence of production and service, of workers and management, the rapid and informal redeployment of staff when and where they are needed are used to cultivate a team spirit. The team is confronted with a common task, serving *quickly and efficiently* an unending stream of hungry and impatient customers; the aim is to satisfy each one of them within four and a half minutes.

Seated behind a one-way mirror in the 'control room', the managers have a panoramic view of the store. Computer terminals in front of them can tell them at the press of a button how many portions of chips, burger-specials or milk-shakes have been sold in any given period, how fast each individual worker has been serving the customers and how much money is in each till. As the queues begin to get longer during peak times, as managers come out to give a helping hand, it is impossible not to feel a sense of *pressure*, whether you are a worker, a manager, a customer or an observer.

The field research

The central headquarters of Fun Food International agreed to allow me to investigate four of the company's London outlets and to interview management and staff. Practical considerations dictated that I concentrate on three stores in central London. Management in all three stores were extremely helpful, offering me information about their operations and permitting me to interview a number of their staff, in spite of the disruption which this caused. Of course, it was not possible to draw a careful sample; instead I had to interview whoever was available during my visits at off-peak periods. The composition of the workforce, however, proved quite homogeneous, with most staff coming from the same age-groups with similar family and educational backgrounds; this reduces the seriousness of errors due to sampling inadequacies.

TABLE 3.1
Sample of staff interviewed at Fun Food

	Store 1	Store 2	Store 3	All
Management	4	7	4	15
Supervisors	1	4 (1)	2	7 (1)
Staff	9 (5)	10 (4)	7 (1)	26 (10)
TOTAL	14 (5)	21 (5)	13 (1)	48 (11)

Note: Figures in parentheses are staff working for less than 35 hours per week.

The profile of staff at Fun Food could not be more different from those of Michael Lansby and Saint Theresa's. Virtually all of the staff employed in Fun Food's own stores are in their teens or early twenties and management only slightly older. A store manager:

> We *just* have to recruit young people because of the pace of work. Older people couldn't stand the pace ... this job, with its clean, dynamic image, appeals to younger people.

About a third of the workers work part-time and several of them are students; most of them live with their parents and only a small percentage have dependent relatives. For many, it is their first job and very few expect to stay for more than a year: 'I couldn't last here for more than a year but for the time being it is OK. I have a casual approach to the job, my expectations are low and right now the job suits me,' was a comment which typified the attitude of many workers. 'Lasting' was a word used by many of them to describe their feelings to their work.

There were only three female managers (a lower percentage than in the other two establishments) in the sample, but 16 of the 33 non-management staff were women. Thirty-six out of the 48 people I interviewed had been in their jobs for less than one year, although most of the managers had worked in other of the company's stores previously. Eighteen out of the 26 workers I interviewed described their job as the first 'real' or 'proper' job they had had. Nine of

The fun food machine

these workers were students (only one of them in catering), 2 were long-term tourists and 1 had just graduated from university. Five had been through a Youth Training Scheme and 7 had been unemployed prior to taking up their jobs. Only 3 individuals in my entire sample (all managers) were married, and only one had a dependent relative although several had children (not living with them). All but 6 of 33 workers and supervisors lived with relatives (usually mother and/or father).

Ten of the 15 managers in the sample had started as staff members and been promoted, while 5 had moved directly to management positions by virtue of their qualifications or work experience. Two had degrees, 2 had catering qualifications and 1 had a Higher National Diploma. Eight had no qualifications at all beyond high school. Most of them had worked in several of the company's outlets and had been with the company for an average of just over three years; only 4, however, had been with Fun Food for five years or more.

TABLE 3.2
Length of service sample

	M	S	C1	C2	C3	C	All
Less than 1 month	1	0	0	2	3	5	6
1–3 months	1	0	5	1	3	9	10
3–6 months	4	2	1	0	0	1	7
6–12 months	2	3	3	4	1	8	13
1–2 years	3	2	0	2	0	2	7
2 or more years	4	0	0	1	0	1	5
TOTAL	15	7	9	10	7	26	48

M : Management in all three stores
S : Supervisors in all three stores
C1, C2 and C3: Staff in Stores 1, 2 and 3; C: all staff

The sample represented approximately 25 per cent of the workforce of the three stores. Store 1 employed approximately 80 individuals, Store 2, regarded as the company's flagship, 90, and Store 3, opened just over a year before my visit, 40. Between 55 and 65 per cent of staff members were full-time workers. The number of daily transactions in Store 1 averaged 2,200, of which 80 per cent involved a meal. Store 2 was particularly sensitive to the seasonal variations in the tourist trade and it ranged from 2,500 to a remarkable 10,000 transactions daily, of which about 60 per cent involved more than one item. Store 3 ranged from 700 to 1200 transactions daily.

In an attempt to obtain some more information about working in fast food, I talked at length to some 25 of my students with catering experience, most of them in fast food. Most of them also answered the questions on my structured interview schedule. Although this material has not been incorporated in the statistical tables given below, it provides useful insights into some of the practices of fast-food chains, other than Fun Food; for this reason I have quoted some of their views.

Job expectations and job satisfaction – a general view

Two factors stood out as the major work priorities of both management and staff in the sample, good pay and the interest and variety of the job. They were each mentioned by 30 individuals in the sample as being one of the three most important things they expected from their work. But while interest and variety headed the priorities of 13 staff members and supervisors and 5 managers, pay topped the priorities of only 4 staff members and supervisors. Job security was the third most important priority of managers and supervisors, while good workmates was the third priority of staff members. Job security was of virtually no concern to staff members.

Good supervision and good career prospects were hardly mentioned at all. The latter may seem surprising, considering the firm's policy of internal promotions. One of the firm's senior managers at central headquarters said:

> Each and every one of our staff can become a supervisor, or a manager for that matter – provided they show the right attitude and they are prepared to work hard. There are few industries which provide similar career opportunities to young people today.

Few of the workers I interviewed, however, saw promotion as a realistic possibility. One of them said that 'even if you are a hard worker, you have to chase the job, you don't get automatically promoted.' A comment which seemed to sum up the workers' dismissive attitude towards the prospect of promotion was, 'you only get promoted if you are on your knees most of the time.'

The overall degree of job satisfaction was limited. Managers, although the most satisfied of the different groups, expressed less satisfaction than management at Saint Theresa's and Michael

The fun food machine

TABLE 3.3
Evaluation of own job by management and staff

	M	S	C1	C2	C3	C	All
First rate	1	1	1	0	0	1	3
Pretty good	7	3	1	3	2	6	16
So-so	3	1	4	6	2	12	16
Not too good	4	0	2	0	1	3	7
Very bad	0	2	1	1	2	4	6
TOTAL	15	7	9	10	7	26	48

M : Management in all three stores
S : Supervisors in all three stores
C1, C2 and C3: Staff in Stores 1, 2 and 3; C: all staff

Lansby and indeed less than some of the manual workers in these establishments. Workers at Fun Food expressed more dissatisfaction with their work than most other groups in the survey; only 7 out of 26 workers found their jobs better than average and several used the same slang word to describe their work – crap jobs. However, there was a distinct difference between workers in the three stores; dissatisfaction was particularly acute in Store 3 and, to a lesser extent, Store 1.

It comes as no surprise that job dissatisfaction was felt strongest by those managers and staff who wanted, above all else, interesting jobs. Eight of the 15 managers saw interest and variety as one of their two most important priorities; only 2 of these 8 saw their jobs as 'pretty good', while 6 of the remaining 7 saw their jobs as 'pretty good' or better. The same was true of workers. Seventeen of the 26 listed interest and variety as one of their two top expectations; of these 17 only 4 saw their jobs as 'pretty good', while 3 of the remaining 9 saw their job as 'pretty good' or better. Lack of interest and variety was one of the main causes of job dissatisfaction.

This is confirmed by Table 3.4, showing that for a majority of both management and staff the job itself was the main problem. Jackie, one of the most satisfied workers from Store 2, where staff were distinctly happier, had worked for 8 months at Fun Food:

> All in all the job is pretty good for the time being. But you don't feel that you've achieved anything here; I would like a more interesting job in the future, but the atmosphere here is friendly and the hours are OK for me.

Thérèse, a young Frenchwoman, came to London on holiday after

The fun food machine

her first year at law school; she became a member of a religious sect and decided to stay. She had been working at Store 3 for about three months, 15–20 hours per week, while also serving breakfast at a West End hotel. Replying to one of the standard questions, she described her job as completely dull and monotonous. She said:

> I find no fulfilment at all in this job. It is convenient for me and they are helpful letting me work the hours I want, but fulfilment, satisfaction no, not here.

Some of the workers did report a degree of job satisfaction, partly because of the industry's dynamic image; some felt a sense of fun and excitement about working in fast food: 'There is plenty of action and excitement here,' said a young trainee supervisor, but qualified his answer:

> I have made many friends but unfortunately many of the good people here have left – the majority for better jobs. I would

TABLE 3.4
Main problems and main advantages of work at Fun Food

	M	S	C1	C2	C3	C	All
'The main problem with my job is':							
The job itself (*)	9	2	7	4	4	15	25
Hours	12	1	3	1	0	4	17
Pay	1	3	3	0	1	4	8
Management/supervision	0	1	2	2	2	6	7
'The main advantage of my job is':							
Friendly atmosphere (+)	3	1	2	4	1	7	11
Work experience	4	2	1	0	1	2	8
Good/reasonable pay	2	1	2	1	1	4	7
Promotion	5	2	0	0	0	0	7
Hours	1	1	2	1	0	3	5
The job itself	2	1	2	0	0	2	5
Safe job	2	1	0	0	0	0	3

(*) includes answers like 'monotony', 'boredom', 'lack of variety', etc.
(+) includes good workmates

Note: Not everybody answered both questions above, and some people gave more than one answer.

M : Management in all three stores
S : Supervisors in all three stores
C1, C2 and C3: Staff in Stores 1, 2 and 3; C: all staff

The fun food machine

like to move to something more interesting, perhaps being a chef or training in electronics.

For the majority of the management and staff at Fun Food their job offered little intrinsic satisfaction. This, however, seems to contrast with the contents of Table 3.5, which show that a majority of the managers and several of the staff did not find their jobs 'dull and monotonous'. 'Fast food is lively, it is fun, it has the challenge of people,' said one of the store managers, who took both pride and pleasure in his work. However, Firoz, one of the duty managers, who had started as a staff member three and a half years earlier, said:

> None of your statements seems quite right. Although the job is not interesting, once you've got into the routine, you are so busy all the time, you don't feel bored. Only after the end of your shift, you keep asking yourself what you have achieved. ... There is pressure in this job, but no intellectual stimulus.

This comment (which echoes some of the responses in other catering establishments) highlights one problem with the way the question was put; for some people, their work was neither interesting nor boring – it simply allowed them no time to think. Moreover, as some of the earlier comments suggest, for many it was the people who made work interesting, not the intrinsic qualities of the job itself.

TABLE 3.5
How interesting were their own jobs

	M	S	C1	C2	C3	C	All
Interesting all the time	1	1	0	0	0	0	2
Interesting most of the time	10	3	2	6	3	11	24
Mostly dull and monotonous	4	1	6	3	2	11	17
Very dull and monotonous	0	1	1	1	2	4	5
TOTAL	15	7	9	10	7	26	48

M : Management in all three stores
S : Supervisors in all three stores
C1, C2 and C3: Staff in Stores 1, 2 and 3; C: all staff

The workers and their jobs

Fast-food workers generally work in three areas: kitchen, counter and customer areas. Managers make an effort to rotate their staff from area to area, but most of my respondents claimed that they spent most of their time in one – the one to which they were regarded as most suited. Cleaning, sweeping, and tidying the customer areas involves no skill at all, but allows the workers some freedom from direct supervision; they can work at their own speed. In the kitchen the pressure is uneven; the machines, the regulations and the demands from the counter determine what the workers do and how (25 rules regulate the frying of chips alone). On counter, the workers must prove that they can master the stereotyped forms of address (they are often printed on the back of the menu: 'May I help you sir/madam? Would that be *large* french fries? Anything to drink, sir/madam? Enjoy your meal, sir/madam'). They must learn the order in which the various items must be fetched. They must master the company smile. And then it's all down to speed – how quickly they can process the orders.

The Job Index average of Fun Food workers (15.6) compares favourably with that of all manual groups in my survey except for the hospital cooks. The average, however, conceals very significant variations; 5 of the 26 staff scored 20 points or more, while 8 scored 13 or less. All 8 people who scored 17 or more had worked for the company for less than three months. Those with six months' service or more averaged 14.2 on the Job Index. It seems that the longer a worker stays in fast food, the lower the perceived quality of his/her job.

In spite of these variations very few found their jobs enjoyable,

TABLE 3.6
Average Job Index scores at Fun Food

Management:	20.5
Supervisors:	18.3
Staff (Store 1):	14.6
Staff (Store 2):	15.8
Staff (Store 3):	16.8
All staff:	15.6

High score indicates high level of job autonomy (27 = max score)
Low score indicates low level of job autonomy (9 = min score)

and those who did were the most recent recruits. Paradoxically, the ones with the longest service, i.e. the ones who lasted longest, were the ones who experienced less satisfaction in their job. Lorna, after working for a year in Store 1, had moved to Store 3 a year earlier. She had got several O-levels and was now doing her A-levels by correspondence, hoping to start a degree in sociology the following autumn. She said:

> It's just a job. I would like to move to a good job to better myself, perhaps clerical, a job with more interest and responsibility. This job makes me independent and helps me support myself while I'm studying but it has no variety, no skill.

Skill and training are important issues in fast food; most fast-food companies claim to be very serious about skill development and one of them has in seriousness established an international Hamburger University. The staff handbook of System Food, one of Fun Food's main competitors, proclaims: 'It is the goal of System to develop the highest level of skill among employees. Therefore, a common training programme has been established within each restaurant to train and direct staff in the System's methods.' Money is spent lavishly to produce training aids, brochures, video-tapes and multiple-choice tests (How many ice scoops go in a large drink? (Cola/orange) 1 2 3 Tick appropriate one.)

Several of my students had worked for System Food; a small minority were impressed with the training they had been given, but most of them said that training was all in the book, rarely in reality. These are two typical responses:

> The company has a training policy but it is generally not followed through in the store where I work. It is one of the busiest stores and there just is no time to train staff. People I worked with showed me how they did things.

> I started with 10 or 12 others; I was just put on the lobby with people out there. I was left to pick it up by myself. There was never an instance when someone was told to show me. Within about a week I knew the job.

Similar views were expressed by the workers at Fun Food. More than half of the staff members said that within a week they had 'picked up the job' and only one part-time worker said that it took

The fun food machine

him more than a month. Several described the training they had received as inadequate. Nineteen out of the 26 workers in the sample described their jobs as unskilled. Matthew, at 17, was studying for a catering qualification; he had been working at Fun Food for six months, three or four nights per week, a couple of hours per night; he was hoping to move eventually to 'real catering':

> The service here is poor; the staff don't have the right attitude towards the customers. They haven't been taught properly; they should train you better, teach you more about the machines. I don't enjoy the job much, it's boring and disorganized, that's why I can work whatever hours I choose, there is no control.

His views were echoed by an assistant store manager who said 'only when they become supervisors they learn how to operate the machines; before that, all they do is just press buttons'. Sharon was another student who had worked part-time in Store 2 for nearly two years – she was hoping to enter medical school:

> It's not an easy job but it's very monotonous. We have no breaks when we are busy and the heat is bad if you work on production; if there was more variety and skill people here would be less short-tempered. The staff would stay longer too; in this place I've met two or three hundred people who came to work and only five or six of us are still here.

To get through the day, they had to fantasize. Nineteen out of the 26 workers said that they kept their minds on other things while they worked – only working on the till required some concentration. Eric, like Sharon, was a long-term worker in Store 2; he hoped to move to the building industry:

> You soon start daydreaming; you can do the job with your eyes shut. It's a means to an end kind of thing. Most people do it because of the money and the friends; otherwise you can't wait for the break to go back home.

Cecilia had been working in Store 3 for three months, after eight months on the dole. Most of her friends were unemployed, and she confided to me that she kept her job secret from them. She said:

> I am supposed to do 35 hours a week but I take a day off each week. I find some excuse because I don't like working here.

The fun food machine

It's just *so* boring; you have to think about other things to get through each day.

'Playing games' was another way of getting through the day. David had started work only two weeks earlier – a year after completing his youth training programme, and this was his third job. In both of the previous ones he had been made redundant, but was determined to make the best of this job:

> You get a sense of satisfaction if you can serve the customer in four and a half minutes, which is what we aim for. I look at the queue in front of my counter and at the queues in front of the other counters – and try to keep my customers one step ahead of those in the other queues.

Some of the games that workers in fast food described to me were innocent attempts to make the time pass quicker – catching a girl's eye as she enters the store and seeing if she will join your queue. Others were attempts to bend the rules and see what they could get away with. Andrew from Store 3:

> The book says that you should make hamburgers in sixes; you try and make 18 all at once. You should only fry four pieces of fish in the basket; when the manager is not looking, you put five, or six or seven. You constantly try to build up stock by cutting corners. Sometimes, the managers themselves turn a blind eye, because they know that if you didn't cut corners you couldn't keep up with the customers.

One of my students who had worked in System Food confirmed that short-cuts are the rule:

> There is a world of difference between what you are supposed to do and what you do. Everything is down in the book but few things are done according to the book. The machines are sometimes to blame – the buns stick on the inside of the machine, you use the spatula in a special way to get them unstuck. The mustard and ketchup come out of dispensers which you are supposed to handle in a particular way; in practice they get clogged up and as long as you can get them to work it's OK. People become lackadaisical and don't squirt the middle of the bun, some occasionally miss the bun altogether.

And another:

When you are busy, you don't wait for the buns and burgers until they are ready. With the fries, you switch off the frier while they are still frying, so the buzzer won't go off, after you've taken them out. I would go so far as to say that managers do it too; many will keep fries for longer than seven minutes which is the regulation. If they are short of staff and the queues are growing, they will turn a blind eye whatever you do, provided that you keep going.

Undoubtedly breaking the rules and playing games broke the drudgery of work. But as Burawoy has argued (1981:92f; 1985:37ff), while these games restore some degree of control to the workers, they are tolerated and even encouraged by management because they enhance the efficiency of work. Sometimes short-cuts enhance quantity at the expense of quality and management are forced to accept them during a period of high pressure. Then when the pressure subsides they find it impossible to stamp them out.

All in all, it can be argued that short-cuts, games, little trade-secrets and personal touches of the workers represent a little arena of negotiation, a terrain of disputed control, even in industries where Taylorism and technology seek to strip the individual of all control. Huw Beynon has described the great ingenuity with which car workers seek to establish some control over the domination of the assembly line (Beynon, 1973:Ch. 6). Fast-food workers may lack the tradition and industrial organization of car workers, but their youthful enthusiasm compensates. They soon learn that concessions made by management on Saturday cannot be taken away easily on Monday; they realize that once management have taken short-cuts themselves and have been seen to bend the rules themselves, they cannot expect their staff to stick to the letter of the regulations. Even in fast food, with its carefully planned production process and its vigilant management, the workers discover ways of maintaining a measure of autonomy and putting their personal stamp on their work. Several managers responding to my question concerning the quality of the food they produced said that it depended on who was on duty. One of my students exaggerated slightly but was trying to make this point:

> You won't believe this, but I can go to the A-Star store where I've worked, have a 'burger special' and I can tell you who made it – from the amount of seasoning, the place where it has

been put, the way it's been wrapped and many other small details.

It should not, however, be thought that these personal touches had the effect of completely defeating the inherent monotony of work. Paul, at 25, was the oldest worker I interviewed; he had been working in Store 1 for two months after three years in the engineering industry:

> Of course there are short-cuts, of course rules are meant to be broken; but I do feel like a robot sometimes. . . . Only part of me is working here. I would like to do something that would make me feel wholesome.

All in all then few of the staff at Fun Food obtained any intrinsic satisfaction from their jobs; the work was described as monotonous, boring, lacking in creativity, with no room for individual initiative. Few of them felt that they worked in catering. In response to the question 'What do you say when people ask you what you do for a living?' only 4 out of 26 said they worked in catering, 6 said they were students, 8 mentioned the name of the firm, 5 said they worked in fast food, one said she was a sales assistant. Two said that they were unemployed; they didn't want their friends to know that they had jobs!

Pay and workmates

In contrast to fast-food workers' dissatisfaction with intrinsic aspects of their work, the majority expressed varying degrees of satisfaction with their pay, their workmates and the quality of supervision. While up to 60 per cent of the respondents complained about the 'job itself', only 15 per cent saw pay as 'one of the bad things' about working at Fun Food and only 20 per cent complained about supervision. The only group at Fun Food who were unhappy about pay were the supervisors; as this group had longer length of service than staff members, it is possible that pay became a more serious concern the longer staff stayed at Fun Food. The firm was generally thought of as paying slightly above the average rates for the fast-food industry and 3 workers had left their jobs at System Food because of the higher rates paid by Fun Food.

The rates of pay at Fun Food were slightly higher than those of the other catering establishments I visited. Workers mostly on £1.85 per hour earned more than all the manual staff at Michael Lansby and all but the cooks at Saint Theresa's. Even this rate, however, would place them in the bottom 5 per cent of all male manual workers (full-time and over 21) and in the bottom 33 per cent of all female workers (full-time and over 18).[4]

TABLE 3.7
Rates of pay at Fun Food (in £)

	Management	Supervisors	Staff
Net weekly	95–110	55–80	
Hourly		1.90–2.00	1.75–1.95
Gross annual	6,800–8,200		

Note: Management rates do not include those of store managers

The reasons for most workers' relative satisfaction with pay are not difficult to see. 27 out of 33 staff lived 'at home' with family relatives. A number of them made a contribution to the family budget, but as someone told me, 'my money goes on things I like, not on things I need'.

Most of the workers I interviewed earned more than their friends, many of whom were on youth training schemes or unemployed, and their wages gave them a sense of freedom and independence – a year or two earlier most of them were at school, nagging their parents for pocket money. They could now spend 'real money', buying their own cigarettes and drink, clothes and records and being able to afford a good night out with their friends and mates. As Robins and Cohen have argued, however:

> What the youth wage does *not* buy . . . is independence from home. It's only because they go on living with their parents, their subsistence needs subsidized out of the family wage, that young workers can earn less, but still have more to spend on enjoying themselves, than their elders. (1978:8–9)

It is not accidental that only a couple of my respondents living 'at home' had unemployed parents and the majority had both mother and father in jobs subsidizing their day-to-day living. It is highly unlikely that fast-food workers would be satisfied with their pay if they had to support families, pay rents and bills out of their pay packets. Without mum and dad to pick up these costs, it is also

The fun food machine

TABLE 3.8
Friends and work relations at Fun Food

	M	S	C1	C2	C3	C	All
'Have you made any friends since you started working here?'							
Yes	14	7	7	8	6	21	42
No	1	0	2	2	1	5	6
TOTAL	15	7	9	10	7	26	48
'Do you ever meet these friends outside the workplace?'							
Yes	10	5	4	7	2	13	28
No	5	2	5	3	5	13	20
TOTAL	15	7	9	10	7	26	48
'How much do you talk to your workmates at work?'							
A good deal	7	4	5	7	1	13	24
Now and then	8	2	3	3	5	11	21
Hardly at all	0	1	1	0	1	2	3
TOTAL	15	7	9	10	7	26	48
'How would you feel about moving to a similar job but with different people?'							
Fairly upset	2	3	3	7	1	11	16
Not bothered	13	4	6	3	6	15	32
TOTAL	15	7	9	10	7	26	48

M : Management in all three stores
S : Supervisors in all three stores
C1, C2 and C3: Staff in Stores 1, 2 and 3; C: all staff

highly questionable whether fast-food chains would be able to recruit any staff at the rates which they offer.

If the main point of their job was to earn them their own money, what made the job itself bearable and even pleasant was, for a majority, their workmates and the cheerful atmosphere (see Table 3.4). All but 4 individuals said that co-operation and teamwork were good or very good. In spite of the short period most of the workers had been at jobs (management for an average of 18 months, supervisors for an average of 10 months and staff for an average of 7 months) the majority had made some friends at work and a very substantial number met with their friends outside the workplace (a much higher percentage than at the other two establishments). As shown by Table 3.8, several of the workers, including nearly all those with 6 months or more on the job, said they would be fairly upset if they had to move away from the people they worked with. Finally, in spite of the pressure and the pace of work, most workers talked a good deal to each other during work.

Although I found no significant statistical correlation between job satisfaction and the quality of their work relations (as reported in Table 3.8), the workers in Store 2 who reported the highest degree of job satisfaction (Table 3.3) were also happiest about their work relations; they met outside work more, talked to each other more and would be more upset if they moved away from their workmates than workers in the other two stores. Sharon's views again:

> Co-operation among staff is good. Things have improved a lot since Nick [the store manager] came here. Also with some of the managers coming from the staff, like Delroy and Mike, you feel that they care for you; they work *with* you. That's really what has kept me here for two years – meeting people, getting to know them and helping each other.

Len had been a bank clerk for three and a half years before going to university and doing a degree in Economics. He had just finished his studies and had taken up a job in Store 2 in order to finance a trip abroad, two weeks before I interviewed him:

> Teamwork here is *great*. We have a good time, a good laugh and a joke together. In a place like this it's the people who make the job, and the people I've met here are great. I'll stay in touch with a couple after I stop working here.

Managers and their jobs

Managers at Fun Food were only slightly more satisfied with their jobs than the workers. In spite of the fact that only 4 out of the 15 managers found their job dull and monotonous, several complained of a lack of creativity or responsibility in their work. Tim was one of only two managers with catering qualifications; he had been a duty manager at Fun Food for less than a year, but felt disillusioned:

> Since I started working here, I've been feeling worse and worse. The problem with this job is that it lacks creativity. It doesn't really have much to do with catering. Here I am a glorified

The fun food machine

cashier and supervisor; I can't utilize my skills and creativity. I'm giving this job until the summer; then I'll look for something more taxing and rewarding.

Like Tim, Robert had a degree in catering; he went to college after short stints as a clerical officer for the Civil Service and as an insurance salesman. He started at Fun Food a year earlier as a trainee manager; within 3 months he was duty manager and within 7 months he was deputy manager of the company flagship store:

> My qualification comes handy here but it is only relevant for about ten percent of what I do. I need the experience for a year or two and the money is not bad for someone straight out of college. But I would like a job that would stretch me more, with more responsibility.

Diana was another manager who had rapidly earned promotion; an outspoken black woman, she said:

> I would like to settle down in a *constructive* job; a mentally stimulating job. This job makes me want to move out of catering; I wouldn't advise anyone to work here. I am too intelligent for this job.

Managers at Fun Food had a distinctly instrumental attitude towards their job – Fun Food was the stepping stone towards better and more interesting things. Only one of them said that he expected to be with the company five years later. The majority expected to be running their own business (most of them in catering) or to be in senior management in another company. Three, however, said that they would try to move into intrinsically rewarding jobs. Steven had been with the company for five years; he started as a staff member 'to finance a little reggae band' and having been promoted gradually to duty manager, he still saw his job as a short-term prospect:

> I'd go mad if I thought I'd have to work here for ten years. At the moment I have this stupid little dream of making a living by writing songs and playing music. I started here just for the cash to finance my band. I don't really know what my feelings for Fun Food are. It's a good steady job for me, but sometimes I feel used, that I am being used. . . . But then you can't afford to look for interesting jobs these days.

Comments like these display a considerable ambivalence by many of the managers at Fun Food, some would say an almost schizoid attitude, where the job is both good and bad, interesting and boring, fulfilling and alienating. This is reflected in the fact that 10 of the 15 management agreed with the statement that their 'feelings and attitudes towards their jobs and their employer changed frequently with the ups and down of work'. This is a far higher proportion than in the other establishments and suggests that attitudes of those working in fast food change fast.

Few found their jobs intrinsically rewarding and some found them deeply frustrating. Max had been a duty manager in Store 1 for 15 months, having started as a staff member two years earlier. His accent and his passion for cricket suggested a middle-class background:

> What keeps me here? I often ask myself this question; I don't get any genuine satisfaction here. I suppose that I stay here because it is difficult to get a decent job outside which pays as much. I'd never go on the dole, I don't think that people should live off the state, but I'd change it as soon as possible for something more interesting.

Apart from intrinsic aspects of the job, the length of working hours was the main cause of dissatisfaction among managers; most of them averaged 60 hours per week and had on occasions (when short-staffed) to work up to 80 hours per week. Several said that their social and family lives suffered as a result; one of the managers engaged to a duty manager from a different store explained how they only managed to have one or two free days together each month.

How, then, were these long hours at work spent? What did managers do when they managed? Meetings and discussions took about one hour of their time daily, and routine paperwork another one to two hours. As each store had between 3 and 10 new workers each week, a lot of time was spent on recruitment and selection; some managers spent about half their time on selection and training of staff and supervisors. Although the store managers spent about half their time talking to staff and management 'trying to prevent staff problems rather than having to deal with them', 11 of the managers on my sample reported that there was not enough consultation with staff.

By far and away most of the managers' time was spent on supervision. Most managers reported spending about half of their time

The fun food machine

on routine supervision. Gursel, one of the deputy managers, a man who had worked in a franchise outlet for eight years, before starting work in the company's own stores, said:

> Most of my time is spent on supervision; my responsibility is to make sure that every area is running smoothly. I also help out when things get hectic. . . . Sure, I spend a lot of time talking to staff about problems, after the hours of work. During work we are so busy that I can't do it, but I have a talk to them after work, telling them what they've done wrong.

As shown on Table 3.6, Fun Food managers average 20.5 on the Job Index; this contrasts with 19.8 and 20.8 averages for managers at Michael Lansby and Saint Theresa's respectively. However, the similarities of these scores conceal important differences in the functions of managers in these three establishments. While it is true that managers at Saint Theresa's also spent a lot of their time supervising and trouble-shooting, their control was direct and personal. They enjoyed considerable autonomy in their decision-making, they organized, equipped and ran the catering operation as they wished within the parameters of their budget. Moreover, the nature of this operation and the state of industrial relations there gave them considerable arbitrariness in rewarding and punishing workers. The managers in the cook-freeze kitchen of Michael Lansby, on the other hand, were far more tied down by council regulations and the whims of the faceless administrators of Prince Street. In addition, the cook-freeze technology *and* the women's determination to keep the bosses out of the kitchen meant that direct supervision was all but eliminated.

In contrast to the autocratic management of Saint Theresa's and the laissez-faire management of Michael Lansby, management at Fun Food spent a lot of their time ensuring that rules and regulations were being observed and that the pace of work could meet the varying demand. To be sure, managers at Fun Food had some powers; they could hire and fire, they could deploy and redeploy staff, they could assign overtime and recommend promotion. Most of these powers, however, were themselves defined and restricted by rules and regulations laid out by international headquarters. Moreover, the managers themselves were subject to regular supervision by visiting inspectors from headquarters. One of my students put it in these terms:

> At the place I work, managers are the same as us. They don't run the store. Someone else tells them what to do. They don't make any serious decisions; they just follow orders.

Gordon had been a store manager for nine months. He had joined the company two years earlier, after working for three years as an accountant for an oil company; he said:

> I believe that company stores should be run like franchise stores; in practice it doesn't work like this. Here major decisions have to be cleared at every level. You constantly feel that you are being observed by headquarters; they lay down the rules of the game – you just have to make sure they are applied.

Nick had joined Fun Food six years earlier and had been a store manager at Oxford, before being made store manager of the company's flagship store. He said:

> Store managers have limited freedom and other managers have even less; we have no say on what food we produce or how we produce it. Compared to store managers elsewhere, however, I have a lot of freedom. I can choose my management team, I decide how to spend the store budget and I can organize entertainment for staff, nights out, day trips.

These statements indicate that management control at Fun Food resembles what Edwards (1979) has described as 'bureaucratic'. In contrast to the 'simple' (autocratic) control at Saint Theresa's and the 'technical' control at Michael Lansby, control at Fun Food is achieved by ensuring adherence to myriads of rules and regulations which govern the conduct, the appearance and the rights of all those employed by the company, including the managers. Yvonne, a black trainee supervisor said:

> There are so many rules here that you don't know whether you are coming or going. They could give you a warning for a thousand things – and you cannot argue with the rules. If you get two warnings you get the sack. . . . You should be here to see the managers when the area manager visits the store – they are on edge. And we have to clean like mad.

In addition to supervising their subordinates, controlling them and co-ordinating their activities, some of the managers saw themselves as motivators. Unlike most managers in the other two establishments, some of the managers at Fun Food saw it as their job to motivate their subordinates. Nick, the store manager of Store 2, had the vocabulary of human relations at his fingertips:

> Unless you motivate your staff, they quickly become slap-dash and the quality of the service suffers. Money is of course the main motivator; the novelty of working in fast food – it can be fun; a few are motivated by career and promotion opportunities. But the main one is team-spirit, feeling that they belong to a team and that others depend on them to do their job. I spend a lot of my time talking to management and staff trying to make them feel part of a team.

Management and workers

How successful were managers at cultivating a team-spirit? And how did the workers feel towards them? In assessing the relations between management and staff at Fun Food, special allowance had to be made for the fact that each staff member worked under different supervisors and managers in different shifts. Instead of asking them questions about their direct management superior, the questions were phrased so as to refer to 'most managers here'. This elicited some ambivalent responses: 'Most of them are OK, but some are not sincere; one moment you think that you are getting on well with them but then you find that you can't trust them,' said Sharon, who worked in Store 2. On the whole, however, Table 3.9 indicates that staff at Fun Food thought more highly of their managers than the workers of Saint Theresa's or Michael Lansby. A large majority of the staff found managers 'friendly and informal' and on the whole believed that managers were doing a good job.

Although there were certain complaints against specific managers, two of the criticisms were of a more general nature, the arrogant behaviour of a number of managers (especially in Store 3) and the complete lack of consultation. Some staff members felt that the managers' friendliness was only skin-deep; Eric:

> They are friendly on the surface but underneath they don't care about you. If they saw you in the street they wouldn't say hello to you.

Andy, a trainee supervisor, had just 'walked in' and got a job in

TABLE 3.9
Staff attitudes towards management

	M	S	C1	C2	C3	C	All
Most managers here are:							
Friendly and informal	12	2	8	8	3	19	33
Formal and impersonal	2	3	2	1	3	6	11
Pushy and bossy	0	1	1	1	2	4	5
Lackadaisical	1	0	0	0	0	0	1
Two-faced	0	1	0	1	0	1	2

Note: Figures above include some double answers, i.e. 'Some managers are ... and some ...'.

	M	S	C1	C2	C3	C	All
Is management here doing a good job?							
Good job	12	3	5	7	3	15	30
Good job for the store, bad for staff	1	0	2	2	1	5	6
Bad job	1	1	2	1	1	4	6
Don't know/So-so	1	3	0	0	2	2	6
TOTAL	15	7	9	10	7	26	48
Are managers here arrogant towards their staff?							
Yes	0	4	4	5	4	13	17
No	15	3	5	5	1	11	29
Don't know	0	0	0	0	2	2	2
TOTAL	15	7	9	10	7	26	48

Note: The two respondents in Store 3 answering 'Don't know' had not been employed long enough to have formed an opinion.

M : Management in all three stores
S : Supervisors in all three stores
C1, C2 and C3: Staff in Stores 1, 2 and 3; C: all staff

Store 2, a year earlier. A few days before I interviewed him he had learned that he had been accepted in the RAF – the knowledge that he would be leaving Fun Food shortly made his interview quite unlike any of the others; he was effusive and outspoken, looking forward to his new life in the forces. His views towards management were the most extreme I heard:

> They are two-faced; they put on a nice front but if the managers above them shout at them, then they turn at you. They don't try to sort out the problems of staff; they are only interested to get all the work they can out of you.

An equally significant criticism of management concerned the absence of discussions and consultation. Sheila had been working in Store 1 for a year; she was working 20 hours per week, while also studying sociology and psychology at College:

> There has only been one meeting since I came here, a year ago; and even then, they just told us what they had already decided – about uniforms it was.

Alison had been working full-time for ten months, after a short time on the dole; she dreamed of going to Barbados, her parents' country, and starting up as a hairdresser:

> We have had no staff meetings since I came here. They just put up a notice. I feel that we have to take it or leave it, but we can't change things. This is half the problem. If we had a meeting with management we could sort things out before they become big problems. . . . Communication is bad; different managers give me different orders – how can you keep them all happy?

While relations with management were distinctly better than those in Saint Theresa's and Michael Lansby, workers at Fun Food shared the feeling that important decisions were being taken behind their backs, that they had no say on issues which affected them directly. Not one of the supervisors and staff thought there was enough consultation between them and management. Interestingly, 9 of the managers also thought that there was not enough consultation, but a couple said that there was not really enough time for it.

Unions and labour turnover

In fast food, like in traditional mass catering and in cook-freeze, lack of consultation resulted in a climate of mistrust and generated a divide between management and workers. The fact that many of the managers at Fun Food had started as workers narrowed the divide but did not bridge it. Unlike workers in the other two establishments, however, fast-food workers were denied even the elementary sense of influence which trade unions and collective bargaining provide. Sharon again:

> We have no say whatsoever. Everything is on a take it or leave

it basis. You don't like it, you move out. . . . It is difficult to be represented with this labour turnover but of course I would join a union if there was one, I would probably start it.

TABLE 3.10
Staff attitudes towards unions at Fun Food

	M	S	C1	C2	C3	C	All
'We need union protection'							
Agree	6 (2)	6 (4)	7 (5)	5 (5)	3 (2)	15 (12)	27 (18)
Disagree	9	1	2	5	1	8	18
Don't know	0	0	0	0	3	3	3
TOTAL	15	7	9	10	7	26	48
'We need union help over pay and conditions of work'							
Agree	9 (3)	5 (4)	8 (6)	9 (4)	4 (2)	21 (12)	35 (19)
Disagree	6	2	1	1	0	2	10
Don't know	0	0	0	0	3	3	3
TOTAL	15	7	9	10	7	26	48
'If there was a union representing people like me I would join it'							
Agree	7	5	7	8	3	18	30
Disagree	7	2	2	1	2	5	14
Don't know	1	0	0	1	2	3	4
TOTAL	15	7	9	10	7	26	48

Note: Figures in parentheses indicate strong agreement.

M : Management in all three stores
S : Supervisors in all three stores
C1, C2 and C3: Staff in Stores 1, 2 and 3; C: all staff

This view clashes with the popular stereotype of young workers as indifferent or hostile to unionism. Sharon's view, characteristically outspoken, is not isolated. As indicated by Table 3.10, a substantial majority of the staff agreed with the statements that they needed union protection and help over conditions of work and pay. An overwhelming majority said that they would join a trade union if one was prepared to represent them. Of course there were some dissenting voices; David, who had been working in Store 2 for two weeks:

We don't need union protection, they don't exploit you here – when you work late evenings, they pay for a cab to take you

> home. Anyway, I don't like unions all that much, it's a waste
> of time going out on strike.

The majority, however, thought that a union would give them a voice through which to influence their pay and conditions of work. Half of the managers were also positive towards the idea of a union representing them with the company's central management. Most of them felt that they needed help with working conditions, and especially with working hours.

Unions have always regarded the casual nature of much of catering work as the major obstacle to organizing workers in the industry.[5] In fast food, this is compounded by the *temporary orientation* of the workers themselves. This temporary orientation is what sets fast food workers apart from those in the previous two establishments, and influences many of their other expectations and experiences. Most workers found their jobs *suitable for the time being*, most enjoyed certain aspects of their work, but most would find it unbearable if they were stuck in it. And it is this feeling of temporariness which distinguishes Fun Food staff from the workers at Michael Lansby and Saint Theresa's, the majority of whom felt *trapped* in their jobs. Unlike these workers, fast-food workers felt that they *had* a choice. It would be difficult to over-estimate the importance of this factor in shaping workers' experience with their work. John had been working at Store 2 for just under a year, his first 'real job':

> The job suits my needs now but I wouldn't do it for ever. I
> bought my own computer and stereo with what I earn here.
> I'll continue working full-time through the summer and then
> I'll look for a new job, a more interesting job, a job that I
> would enjoy doing 24 hours a day.

Even the alternative of the dole was perceived as an alternative; Yvonne, the supervisor from Store 3:

> I was all right on the dole, but I nagged my mum and she
> nagged me; for the time being it's better than the dole. I'll
> quit when I've had enough.

Working in a 'crap job' and being on the dole were two sides of the same coin for many of the workers I talked to. Andy, talking to me a few days before joining the forces:

> I was bored at home, but I'd rather go back on the dole than

stay here much longer. Nothing really exciting happens here.
It's just all right for a short time.

Most of the workers talked explicitly about their casual and temporary attitude, sometimes using these words. Steven, who rated his job as 'very bad', said:

I've been here for 7 months and it's already too long. This job is good for a couple of months but then you get fed up. It ties you down, especially the weekend work.

And Joyce, a 22-year-old Australian, who had also been working for 7 months, said:

It suits me because I don't have high expectations. I couldn't last here for a year but for the time being it's OK. I have a casual approach to the job.

Drifting in and out of jobs, waiting and hoping to land the plum job is almost a way of life for many of these workers, as their expectations are constantly trimmed by the realities of the job market. The workers at Saint Theresa's and Michael Lansby, whose hopes and aspirations have been lowered by years of marriage and routine, dreamed of winning the pools. The dreams of the fast-food workers had a much greater urgency and power – they dreamed of landing a record contract, of turning professional in sport, of starting a computer business, of romance and glamour. These dreams helped reconcile them to their actual work situation. Above such dreams many of these young workers clung to a more powerful illusion, the illusion of choice. *Even* the long-term staff regard their jobs as short term. Only a handful of the supervisors and staff expected to be in the same job a year later and not one expected to be working for Fun Food in five years' time; only 4 of these 33 people expected to be working in the catering industry at all.

Free of family obligations, free of duties and responsibilities, most Fun Food workers felt that they had some control over their lives. Even though, more than other groups, they considered their jobs intrinsically unrewarding, allowing them to make few decisions, they felt that they could make the most important decision, whether to leave or stay. For them unemployment represented neither a disaster nor a stigma: 'When I'm asked what I do for a living I say that I don't work. I don't like telling people I'm working.' And this feeling of choice is what made their jobs 'bearable', 'suitable' or 'allright'.

This temporary attitude towards work explains in my view the workers' reluctance to take promotion seriously (in spite of management's determined efforts). It also explains why, in spite of the great emphasis that staff place on workmates, less than half said that they would feel upset about moving away from the people with whom they worked. The feeling of temporariness spills outside the workplace; Lorna from Store 3:

> I have no real plans; perhaps I will move to a clerical job or if I pass my exams I could move to computing. But who can make plans these days? I can only plan from day to day.

Her views are echoed by Helen, an 18-year-old who had been unemployed since she left school, interviewed by David Robins:

> I've got no *ambitions*, just one ambition, to get a job. I used to cry at night when I was a kid, thinking about it, that there is no future. No young person these days thinks they'll live till they're old . . . (1984:144)

Instead of planning for the future, most of the young people I interviewed working in fast food looked for short-term solutions to the problems of life, just like the young people who break from the family strait-jacket and drift inexorably towards the seaside towns of the south, earning them their nickname as the Costa del Dole:

> These young people [have] found a way of escaping from the dependence and constraints of family life, and enjoying some kind of autonomy not linked to the wage. But most of them made it clear that they regarded this as a temporary expedient, and also a way of combining a holiday with the search for work. For it is worth remembering that the economy of seaside towns still requires a seasonal influx of unskilled casual labour to staff its hotel, catering and entertainment trades. (Cohen, 1985:35)

The casual and temporary attitude of young workers is not without its ambivalence and conflict. On the one hand, an intense experience of being controlled, observed and assessed which makes even school resemble a playground; on the other hand, a liberating knowledge that they can leave any time they like. On the one hand, a denial of the individuality and creativity, on the other hand, an ability to afford hi-fi and computers; on the one hand, boredom and monotony, on the other hand, companionship and 'fun'.

This ambivalence makes for an extreme volatility of feelings, which I observed repeatedly. I talked to Lauraine, a 16-year-old school-leaver in Store 3 on her fourth day of work. She found her new job 'first rate' and interesting most of the time, especially when she compared it with her only previous job, part-time shop assistant for three months. Her only problem was that her dad did not like her working in the West End. A week later, she confided, 'I really don't like it here; the work is so boring, I can't bear it.' She agreed to answer the interview questions again and she now found her work completely dull and monotonous. Although she had only started work two hours earlier, she said with an intensity of despair I only encountered at Saint Theresa's 'I just can't wait for my dad to come and take me home.' She left a few days later.

Another result of the workers' ambivalent feelings towards their job is the radical change of attitudes for the worse as soon as they left the firm. I have already quoted at length Andy's passionate hate for his job, his employer and management, fostered by his imminent new start at the RAF. Similar feelings were expressed by John, one of the kitchen-porters at Saint Theresa's, who had previously worked in a hamburger store of a different chain, A-Star.

> In fast food you don't have time to think about anything else, you have to rush all the time. The job is the same all the time and you get few breaks. The only good thing there was teamwork; you had to stick together. Most people who have left A-Star would agree with me that it's a boring, badly paid, very bad job; but people working there may be scared to say so.

Moving from one fast-food chain to another frequently had the same effect: strong negative feelings towards the previous employer. One of my respondents had previously worked for Fun Food's major competitor, and he described his experience there in this way:

> At System Food they put too much influence on people, they get them to believe that if there is a World War III, System will win it. They brainwash people; when I worked there, we had to follow the manual word for word. You had to be an organization man one hundred percent.

Several of my students who had previously worked in different

The fun food machine

fast-food chains confirmed that after they stopped working, they just wanted to forget all about their experience; they rarely kept in touch with their mates from work:

> I went to their party after I left work there last Friday, but I wouldn't stay in touch if I didn't work there. It's a bit like school, you don't keep in touch with many – you tend to push the whole thing to the back of your mind.

> I've never been back since I stopped working there; to tell you the truth I even avoid walking past it. I just try to avoid everything to do with it.

Such views reinforce the argument concerning the volatility and ambivalence of the attitudes and feelings at Fun Food. While working for Fun Food, the negative attitudes are recognized but held in check by the belief that the door is open; when, however, you have left, this check no longer functions and negative attitudes frequently turn into powerful negative feelings. Hostility then replaces ambivalence.

What can we conclude about the attitudes and feelings of workers at Fun Food? Although they had no serious misgivings about working conditions, management or indeed pay, the majority found their jobs dull and unrewarding. Promotion did not seem to most staff as a realistic or as a desirable prospect, although to company management it seemed as one of the main advantages they offered. If promotion was not important, the intrinsic qualities of work, interest, variety and independence, were all features highly valued by workers and by management alike. It was, however, these qualities which most people found lacking in their work and as a result their job evaluation was among the lowest in my sample, on par with that of the cook-freeze staff, another group in high-tech catering. What made the jobs bearable and for some people enjoyable was their workmates and the pleasant atmosphere.

As in the craft-work environment of Saint Theresa's and the mixed work environment of Michael Lansby, technology at Fun Food was a dominant influence on staff's feelings and attitudes. As in the other two establishments, however, technology has to be studied in conjunction with the social and economic background of the workers, their ages and family conditions, their ambitions and expectations, as well as with the general economic and social climate. In both cook-freeze and fast food, technology seemed to empty jobs of their interest and scope. At the same time, however, individuals' determination to by-pass or overcome or 'humanize' technology was evident everywhere. Like manufacturing workers, therefore, catering workers must be seen not as passive victims of a technological environment but as social beings striving to influence and control this environment.

Fast food, technology and young workers

Nor should technology be seen as a metaphysical force pursuing its own immutable objectives. In fast food, as in capitalist production in general, new technologies are introduced not without opposition in order to increase the profitability of capital and to reduce reliance on the workers' skills, abilities and willingness to work. New technologies do not amount merely to new machines but rather to new relations between men and machines and new relations among people at the workplace. Contrary to System Food's trite propaganda ('It is the goal of System to develop the highest level of skills among employees'), Henry Ford very clearly saw technology as a way of addressing 'the pressing need to take away the necessity for skill in any job done by anyone' (1923:102).

In recent times, Professor Theodore Levitt has been the most uninhibited and outspoken advocate for the introduction of Fordist techniques into catering. If cook-freeze turns a kitchen into a factory, the fast-food outlet

> is a machine that produces, with the help of totally unskilled machine tenders, a highly polished product. Through painstaking attention to total design and facilities planning, everything is built integrally into the machine itself, into the technology of the system. The only choice available to the attendant is to operate it exactly as the designers intended. (1972:46)

While my respondents' comments on short-cuts, games and trade secrets contradict the claim that fast-food technology totally eliminates the human factor from catering, Levitt's statement describes clearly the rationale behind it.

If technocratic management has only been making its mark on catering for the past twenty years or so, some sections of the working classes of capitalist countries have felt its effects as well as confronted

it over a far longer period. These effects are clearly outlined by
Andre Gorz:

> It makes no difference to proletarians what they produce or
> what they work for. They have been stripped of all autonomous
> capacities by capital and compelled to work 'with the immutable
> regularity of a giant automaton'. . . . The entire manufacturing
> process has been thought out once and for all by specialists
> whose technical intelligence is embodied in the organization of
> the workshop. The very meaning of the notion of work is
> changed. It is no longer the workers who work the machines
> and adjust their actions and movements to obtain the desired
> result. Rather they are being worked on by the machinery.
> The result of their labour is already there, rigorously
> programmed, expecting to be produced; the machine is pre-
> set, requiring a succession of simple regular motions. The
> mechanized system does the work; you merely lend it your
> body, your brains and your time in order to get the work done.
> (1982:38)

But, as work is stripped of creativity, individuality and imagination for large sections of the population, a contempt for work emerges. Many of the young workers at Fun Food had already developed this contempt for the work they did ('crap jobs').[6] According to Willis, an entire educational counter-culture has emerged, preparing the youngsters for intrinsically unrewarding jobs:

> Most work – or the 'grafting' they accept they will face – is
> equilibrated by the overwhelming need for instant money, the
> assumption that all work is unpleasant and that what really
> matters is the potential particular work situations hold for self
> and particularly masculine expression, diversions and 'laffs' as
> learnt creatively in the counter-school culture. These things
> are quite separate from the intrinsic nature of any task. (Willis,
> 1978:100)

To be sure fast food has little to offer in the way of 'masculine expression' – it does, however, have most of the other attributes; above all it has instant money. In a period of youth unemployment crisis, it is hard cash rather than the industry's glamour and dynamism which attracts boys and girls to fast-food jobs. Equally, however, the fast-food industry is attracted to the 'green' labour of young boys and girls, whose agile limbs and alert minds can be recruited at a minimum cost[7] and with a minimum of opposition. Above all, their contempt for work has not yet been transformed into active or passive opposition to those who provide it.

If the recipe for the phenomenal international growth and success of fast food rests on the planning and standardization of its methods and the glamorizing of its product, *the recipe's indispensable ingredient is cheap, unskilled young labour*. It is not an exaggeration to say that the systematic exploitation of teenage labour is an even more fundamental feature of fast food than either the rationalization of its production techniques or the marketing of its products. Just try to imagine the workers from Saint Theresa's or Michael Lansby operating a fast-food outlet – the sheer impossibility of this happening illustrates how essential teenage labour is for the fast-food trade. When I suggested to some of the managers that they might try to recruit more dependable and more dependent older people, I was faced with expressions of stunned incomprehension. Nick, the store manager of Store 2:

> Really it would be impossible even to get started. We just *have* to recruit young people because of the pace of work. Older people couldn't stand the pace, they are not energetic enough and they would bring bad habits to the workplace.

While many of the young workers may arrive without bad habits, they are not slow developing them. Gursel, the deputy manager who spent most of his time on supervision:

> This type of job suits the younger people but they eventually tend to become lax and irresponsible. We have a fair level of staff turnover; only a couple have been here since the store opened – on average they stay for six to eight months. Most of them choose to leave, but about one third get the sack.

Managers at Fun Food regarded staff turnover as their major headache. All store managers said that they were chronically short-staffed and that they spent an inordinate amount of time on recruiting and training staff. Jobs were advertised in the evening paper and in Job Centres, but a considerable number went to people who called directly to the stores. Although the precise figures varied from store to store, on average between 40 and 70 per cent of new recruits left within a month and more than 90 per cent left within a year.

Some managers felt that better selection procedures could improve the situation. Nick:

> The reason for our high labour turnover is that we are not choosy enough. At the moment we are so short of staff that we have to accept people who are unsuitable. The rates of pay are one source of dissatisfaction. Some of them are not used to hard work and find it hard to accept the discipline.

As it was, management interviewed about ten applicants for every one they recruited; the interviews, five-minute, informal ones, can hardly be seen as an adequate recruitment tool. But while a more thorough selection procedure could lower the turnover rate, it seems totally unlikely that it could eliminate it. Labour turnover is the inevitable price which fast-food management must pay for recruiting among young people. It is the inevitable consequence of providing jobs devoid of meaning ('crap jobs' in the young people's argot) to youngsters with a casual and temporary orientation towards work and of taking advantage of their subsidized living to offer them low wages.[8] Paul, the worker who confided that he felt 'like a robot sometimes' and wished to do something which made him feel 'wholesome', should have the last word:

> There is a lot of exploitation in the way they pay their staff. It would be better to employ fewer staff, give them better conditions, better hours, better job security and pay them more to give them incentives. As things are now people get fed up after a couple of months; they feel the job ties them down without offering them any long term prospects.

CHAPTER 4
Craft cooking for gentlemen

> My husband was made redundant last year. Since then we've had to make do on my wages – it's been hard . . . I now accept not being able to afford important things in life. But you do get frustrated at times, especially when the children ask for something which you can't give them.
>
> Moira O'Sullivan, mother of two,
catering assistant at Saint George's Club

Nothing is further removed from the brash, neon-lit fantasy world of fast food than the comfortable opulence of a gentlemen's club. That they are part of the same trade is an indicator of the unique diversity of catering. If the fast-food outlet is the product of meticulous planning and assiduous marketing, the gentlemen's club is a lasting anachronism in the world of catering. It is not just the embodiment of tradition but a true time capsule from the heroic age of capital, when business deals were hammered out in oak-panelled smoke-rooms, after a hearty meal. Gentlemen's clubs took the tradition of cooking for sophisticated palates out of the noble households into the public domain of the bourgeoisie. The species has since evolved into the haute cuisine restaurant where many of today's business deals are sealed on company accounts. Chivers:

> The beginnings of the trade of the elaborate menu can be traced back to the clubs for gentlemen and nobility which date from eighteenth century. Only certain of these clubs took on dining as their principal function, but those that did, succeeded in attracting some of the leading French and other Continental cooks from the wealthy households. (1972:643)

I decided to investigate one such club, precisely as the embodiment of tradition in catering, partly cushioned from the ravages of the market-place, partly under the pressures of a changing world where gentlemen are becoming an endangered species. How is such a club surviving the social and economic changes of recent years, the changes in eating and catering habits and the changes in the labour market? And is it possible to find in such an establishment workers who meet the stereotype of the happy artisan, content with his/her age-old trade and craft secrets?

Saint George's Club is the older of the two surviving gentlemen's clubs in one of the Midlands' largest cities. It was started in 1859 when one of its founders became fed up with the food provided at the local inn. It is situated in comfortable Georgian premises in a quiet square not far from the city centre and has over 140 male members, drawn mostly from the city's professional, business and financial circles. The club offers a range of recreational facilities, including two snooker tables, a bridge room, a reading room, a smoke-room and a bar. It also offers some social functions such as golfing events. The club's main purpose, however, is the provision of lunches in an impressive dining-room which seats 60 or more people and catering for a few private evening functions. The club seeks to generate an 'atmosphere of genial fellowship', as its handbook puts it, based on numerous customs and traditions which are cheerfully adhered to. These cover matters such as the members' attire, the order of seating and serving of the meals, the 'procedures at the table', and the items on the menu. The club's revenue comes from members' subscriptions (about £150 annually), bar-takings and property lettings; in addition, members and their guests are charged a flat price of £4.50 per meal. Private functions for members or organizations, such as the Law Society, are paid for separately on an individual basis.

The meals are served promptly at 1 p.m. five days a week and represent a combination of traditional English cooking and the club's own traditions. The menu is made up of a choice of three starters (always including a soup), a choice of two main courses, one of which is always a joint carved at the table, and a choice of three vegetables always including peas. On Fridays the joint is always roast beef and the alternative dish is always plaice. The main course is followed by a selection of sweets, one of which is always hot; as part of the club's tradition, two rice puddings are always served. These are followed by cheese (always including cheddar) and biscuits; finally, the club's members and their guests have coffee in the Smoke-Room, the tradition being that the first member to leave the table and go to the Smoke-Room pays for all the coffees and 'is suitably thanked'. Members can entertain guests at the club and a friendly but businesslike atmosphere prevails. Conversation is lively and revolves around many of the members' shared interests – political and religious discussions, however, are avoided.

The club is run by a housekeeper appointed by the Club Committee, and six female staff, who include a cook and an assistant cook, a head waitress and an assistant waitress and two cleaning women, one for the ground-floor kitchen and one for the dining-room on the first floor.[1] I spent a few days at the club, talking to the staff members, observing the preparation of the meals, and sitting at the table as a guest of one of the club's members. The club was going through a difficult period, partly due to the economic recession and partly because, in the housekeeper's words, 'younger members don't always like a large meal in mid-day'. The number of lunch attendances had dropped from 25 or 30 to about 20 over a five-year period and the menu had been simplified by reducing the choice of main courses from three to two. In an attempt to reduce costs, one member of staff had not been replaced and the kitchen staff was put on a four-day week, so that on Monday, Tuesday and Wednesday only five were present. This meant that a more flexible work arrangement had been worked out; on Mondays, the assistant cook cooked the main course, while on Tuesday the kitchen washing and cleaning lady prepared the vegetable dishes.

The housekeeper, Mrs Felicity Wright, lived on the club's premises. A highly competent woman, she had been with the club for thirteen years after working in a variety of clerical jobs. Her responsibilities included every aspect of management, including ordering, accounts, membership, maintenance of the premises, and staff. She was directly accountable to the Club's Committee but felt that she had a virtually free hand in running the club.

> I love this job, it's totally unique. Where else would you get a club in which every member has a key to the premises and is my boss? And yet, where they all treat you with trust and respect? ... I'm in complete charge, being responsible for cash, stocks, staff and relations with our members. There is so much to my job that you keep learning new things all the time. It's

a challenge, keeping everyone satisfied, everything in order. But it is all done with a smile and the atmosphere is always pleasant.

The 6 women working for the club were all married, aged between 35 and 65, with children of school age or older. All but 1 had been with the club for more than five years and worked for 20 to 25 hours per week each. Like the women at Michael Lansby, these 6 women had long battled with the realities of family and work. Between them they had 18 children and only 2 of them had husbands in jobs. Two of them had previously worked in factories but all of them had done catering or cleaning work, in hotels, school-meals, works canteens and car showrooms. They all liked cooking, but had no formal cooking qualifications.

The kitchen comprised two large, well-ventilated rooms; the equipment was quite old and not in good working order. The cook had repeatedly complained about the ovens, whose temperature controls were defective, but had been told that in the present economic climate they could not be replaced. The only recently acquired piece of equipment was a deep-freezer, which had significantly altered cooking practices; meat was delivered in bulk and kept in store until required and a larger selection of frozen vegetables could be kept.

The deep-freezer also helped the housekeeper and the staff to deal with the major day-to-day problem – the difficulty of predicting the number of members who would have lunch at the club. The housekeeper was instructed to cater for 23 people daily, but the number varied from 10 to 40, and the catering staff had to be prepared to cope. Over a four-month period the average number of individuals having lunch was 20, but about once per week the number rose to over 30 and equally often it dropped to under 15. This created obvious planning problems with which Mrs Wright and Sarah Fowles, the cook, had to deal. Mrs Wright:

> During the half hour before lunch, I judge how many people will be eating by the number of members drinking at the bar. I then tell Sarah if she needs to cook some extra vegetables or sweet. We just have to play it by ear, from day to day. Sometimes I tell the Chairman [who carves the joint at the table] how big the portions should be. Our members also co-operate if I ask them to have the alternative course.

The alternative course itself helped to make use of the left-overs of previous meals; no secret was made of the fact that cottage pies and rissoles were made from the left-over of a joint eaten earlier in the week, that uneaten boiled potatoes often reappeared as sautéed potatoes, or that today's bubble and squeak used up yesterday's leftovers. In this way, with skill and imagination, the supply of meals was made to match the unpredictable demand. Sarah Fowles:

> We waste very little; it's amazing how we cope considering we don't know how many to expect from day to day. But we use our judgement, just like a good housewife makes sure that nothing gets thrown away.

Careful husbanding of resources, flexible work arrangements and excellent teamwork among the staff were seen by Mrs Wright as essential for the continuing success of the club:

> Teamwork is excellent and the staff do a lot more for the club than is expected, for example, they do some of the shopping for the club. I like them a lot, but I don't like to be too friendly with them. I have to be in charge and there are times when I must tell them what to do. We don't mix socially.

These views were echoed by all the members of the staff, who said that they were pleased with the teamwork and liked their work-colleagues. Although they did not mix socially, they all told me that they would be 'fairly upset' or 'very upset' if they had to move to a similar job but working with a different group of people. Likewise, they were all satisfied with the management style of the housekeeper who they found friendly and informal, and 5 of the 6 staff members felt that there was sufficient consultation before important decisions. Unlike most workers in the three large catering operations described earlier, these women did not feel that important decisions were being made behind their back. Even if they could not always affect these decisions, the workers did not feel threatened by invisible forces and a conspiracy of silence as did so many of their counterparts in the larger catering establishments.

Turning to the women's attitudes and orientations towards their jobs, I again found a considerable degree of agreement on most issues. First of all, the job was an important part of their life, both for the money it earned them and as part of their personal identity. Pay ranked after working conditions and good workmates as a top priority in the list of expectations. Mrs Crompton, who had worked in school-meals for twelve years before taking up a waitressing job at Saint George's five years earlier, said:

> My job is very important for me. I once decided to stay at home, we could afford it then, but I soon got fed up. You are more active and independent going to work. I enjoy it, I like the people I work with; we have a little laugh. And the [Club] members show appreciation and interest ... The money is important too.

Most women compared their work at Saint George's favourably to previous jobs. Helen Nicholas, the assistant cook, had cooked for eighteen years at a College of Further Education, when she was made redundant as a result of technical rationalization:

> I used to work at the College; they went to fast food there, micro-wave ovens, frozen food and all that. We used to have a very old-fashioned kitchen which they replaced with a small modern one. They sacked 14 out of the 18 staff, and I got £2,000 redundancy money. I was unemployed for 5 months and started getting tense and nervous, but I was lucky to get this job. ... I prefer this place for the quality of the food [which she cooks] and the atmosphere. At the College I would have stayed there; I had got myself in a rut. It took the redundancy to shake me out of it. I've been very happy since I came here.

On the whole, all 7 women found their jobs enjoyable. In response to my question 'What keeps you in this job?' *not one* of them answered in the manner which was common at the other establishments. Instead of saying that 'It's just a job' or that they worked 'just for the money', they all said that they liked or enjoyed the work or some aspect of it. Four of them found their work interesting all the time and the remaining 3 found it interesting most of the time; all but one felt safe in their job and none thought it too simple. Although for most of them each day was much the same as the next, they didn't mind the routine. They all felt that they made an important contribution to the running of the club and that the standard of the meals and of the service depended on them. They felt that the members of the club showed their appreciation to them and took an interest in their well-being. All the scores on the Job Quality Index were over 15, high compared to other establishments, with the housekeeper and the cook scoring over 20. All the women were satisfied with the working conditions, but 4 mentioned that the work was hard and all 7 felt tired at the end of their 5 to 6-hour day.

Pay

The only serious source of dissatisfaction among the staff was pay. The rates of pay were set just above the rates of the Wages Council and ranged from £1.47 to £1.75 per hour. The women took home between £25 and £40 per week, which was an important part of their family budget. Only 2 of them had working husbands, 1 was divorced, 1 widowed and 2 had husbands on the dole. They all experienced some difficulty in making ends meet, more so than the women in Saint Theresa's and Michael Lansby. For 2 of them money was a cause of deep anxiety; Moira O'Sullivan liked her job as a waitress, but, responding to my question on her family's eating habits, she confessed:

> We used to have fish and chips once a week, but not now, it's too dear. We only have [red] meat about once a month, chicken a bit more regularly. I prefer to cook a pie, something that goes around further. We've been trying to save for a long time for a holiday; we don't go out at all.

Another 3 of the women said that they found it difficult to make ends meet and could not afford at home the kind of food they would like for themselves and their families.

In the light of these difficulties, it is not surprising that 3 of the women expressed dissatisfaction with their pay. 'Pay is not too good here, but I am happy with my workmates and working conditions', said one, and another, 'the rate of pay is bad, especially for the amount of work that you have to do. It can be hard work, like carrying heavy deliveries to the cellar. I wouldn't recommend it to anyone because of the money.' Perhaps more surprising, 1 of the women expressed some dissatisfaction with the differentials between the different grades, especially since the introduction of flexible work arrangements which meant that the assistant cook prepared the main meal on one day, the washing up lady prepared the vegetables, etc.

> Twice per week I have to work in the kitchen doing the cooking [tasks above her official job title] but the cook gets paid more.

So I don't think this is fair. We all do two jobs now, yet we have different rates. They should compensate us for doing more than one job. I would not recommend it to my daughter, unless she knew she was going to do several tasks.

Two women thought that a trade union could help them achieve better pay, but 3 said that a union would be inappropriate in such a small place. 'This is not a place for unions, really, this is a family affair,' said one of the cooks.

These reservations concerning pay contrast with the very few complaints about pay which I heard in the three larger establishments of my survey. This, however, is probably due to the fact that unlike in those three establishments, the staff at Saint George's had no complaints concerning supervision, working hours or the jobs themselves; pay stood out as the only cause of dissatisfaction. The overall job evaluation by the staff at Saint George's was very high, with 2 women regarding their jobs as 'first rate' and 3 as 'pretty good'. One woman thought her job was 'so-so' and only 1 'not too good'. Only 2 of them said that they were keeping their eyes open for a better-paid job.

Nor did the obvious clash between the affluence of the club's membership and the workers' financial troubles at home lead to overt class antagonisms. On the contrary, all the women spoke with affection for the club's members; for instance, one of the waitresses said:

You meet very nice people here; they say 'thank you' to you and treat you with respect. Sometimes, if you have a personal difficulty, they will offer to help you – like using their connections for you.

These positive feelings extended to their attitude towards Mrs Wright. Mrs Owen, one of the two cleaning ladies, who described her job as 'first rate', said:

I really enjoy this job; it's a small place and I like it, the employers are sympathetic and look after you. Mrs Wright, you can talk and explain things to her. She doesn't brush you away.

It is perhaps surprising that, although several women expressed dissatisfaction with their pay, only 1 of them saw poor pay as the fault of her employers. She said:

The rate of pay is bad, especially for the amount of hard work that you have to do. If a better-paid job came up I would take it. Shop work, for example. I've applied for a job at the Co-op – they pay 30 pence more than I get here.

Craft identity and skill

The remaining women, however, seemed to accept low pay as something quite inevitable, a reflection of a woman's limited market power in 'traditional' female jobs – women's jobs don't pay, and cooking, waitressing, cleaning and washing up, whether for school-kids or gentlemen, are very definitely women's jobs. It is perhaps surprising that none of the women thought that she deserved more money because of the skill involved in her work. While all of them took a pride in their work, their lack of a common training programme or tradition precluded a craft identity. They identified with each other as women and workers, as mothers and wives, as neighbours and middle-aged, but not as catering workers, let alone as skilled craftswomen. This is illustrated by the divergence of opinions concerning the degree of skill involved in their work. Three women described their work as semi-skilled, 2 as skilled and 2 as unskilled; however, there was no correlation between the women's actual position and their assessment of the skill involved – for example, one of the cleaning women described herself as skilled, while neither the head waitress nor the head cook did so. It was clear that they each used different criteria to define skill. Sarah Fowles said:

> I've always known how to cook; it's not as if I was specially trained for this job. Most women could do it, it's so like what we all do at home for our husbands and our sons.

It is extremely doubtful whether 'most women' could cook three starters and two high quality main courses, several vegetables and sweet dishes for between 10 and 30 men day in day out, always ensuring that there was enough food but not too much. To be sure no 'fancy recipes' were tried: 'Our members have rather conservative tastes,' said Mrs Wright, 'they like traditional British cuisine, nothing too exotic.' Even so, to me it seemed evident that several of the women were undervaluing their skills. Only Mrs Owen, one of the two cleaning ladies, seemed clear about the skill required in her work:

> It's a skilled job. You can't just come in and do it; you have to keep very high standards. The way the food is presented is important; they way that you present yourself is also important. You need an ability in dealing with people. You can't just shove the food in front of them, you have to make sure that they enjoy their meal.

Apart from the trained cooks at Saint Theresa's, this woman is one of the very few people I interviewed who expressed themselves confidently about *catering skills*. George Orwell has memorably described these skills, as he observed them in a pretentious Parisian hotel in the 1930s. The waiter walks out of the pandemonium of a dirty, noisy, ill-tempered kitchen; he sails across the dining-room 'dish in hand, graceful as a swan' and bows reverently to a customer. And the cook, in that same dirty, noisy, ill-tempered kitchen, generates on plates the illusion of a culinary masterpieces.

At Saint George's Club Gallic pretension is replaced by sound British craftsmanship. It is interesting, however, that even among staff producing a high-quality meal, to be consumed according to elaborate canons of etiquette by an elite clientele, there was no trace of a craft identity. Perhaps the fact that all staff were women lacking formal training and working part-time tended to undermine in their own eyes the scope and value of their work. The fact that they had all worked in jobs outside catering, as cleaners, as shopkeepers and sales assistants, as chambermaids and as factory operatives, made working for Saint George's 'just another job', a good job for the most part, but a job all the same.

The concept of 'skill' has been at the centre of a considerable controversy, since Braverman first forcibly put forward the idea that twentieth-century capitalism has systematically deskilled the worker, stripping him/her of all creativity and initiative. If the high-tech cooking of cook-freeze and fast food provide ample support for the view that modern management is engaged permanently in a struggle to reduce the worker to the role of an appendage of the machine, the traditional catering of Saint George's does not quite coincide with an oasis of artisanship. In both high-tech and traditional set-ups, the workers saw themselves essentially as low-pay, low-skill labour. This, I think, reinforces the views of those who have argued that skill is to an extent socially constructed.[2]

What the women at Saint George's possessed was what Manwaring and Wood (1984) call 'tacit skills', indeed they possessed extensive tacit skills, without which the club could not function. Tacit skill is that 'taken-for-granted skill' of roasting a joint, frying 15 pieces of plaice, preparing a soup, a salad, a sherry trifle, two rice puddings simultaneously, and making sure that they are all ready on the dot of 1 o'clock. It is the skill of cooking for an indeterminate number of people and not throwing food away. These tacit skills may be not learned through formal traineeships, but they are learned all the same and involve the worker's judgment and intelligence, sensitivity and subjectivity.[3]

What the women at Saint George's had not achieved is the transformation of these tacit skills into marketable skills and market power. In fact, their skills, along those of many other women working in catering, went virtually unrecognized by everyone including themselves. Lacking any form of industrial organization or tradition, they were easily swayed to the powerful view that 'any woman' could do their job. Their very identification with other working women, trying to reconcile the demands of low-paid work on the job and unpaid housework at home, made them under-value the uniqueness of their own skills.

Moreover, in a period when unemployment confronted them as part of everyday reality, they saw low pay as the inevitable price of having a job at all, let alone a pleasant job in a friendly place. They concentrated on the positive aspects of their work, the working conditions, the companionship, the members' appreciation and the informal and relaxed atmosphere.

At Saint George's, there is no question of technology determining or even influencing the workers' world. Most of my questions concerning technology and machines were answered as if these belonged to a different world, a world outside Saint George's. 'We use very simple machines here,' I was told again and again, 'the kind of thing we all use at home.' In contrast, however, to technology, size was an extremely significant influence on the workers' work experience. Unlike the workers in Saint Theresa's, Michael Lansby and Fun Food, the women at Saint George's worked in an organization without formal management hierarchy, no direct supervision, with few rules and regulations. Relations among them were wholly personal and informal and this applied to authority relations as well. Problems and grievances were discussed informally and resolved in an ad hoc way. Ingham (1967) and others have rightly pointed out that size affects the degree of bureaucracy in an organization and is, therefore, a paramount influence on the lives of those working. Six of the 7 women (all of whom had earlier worked for larger bureaucratic organizations) at Saint George's explicitly said that they enjoyed the personal quality of work at the Club:

> I love this job, the club is almost like home – you know everyone, you feel natural; not like at Whyte's [large supermarket chain], where it was all formal and you didn't know half of the people you worked with, let alone the customers. Here, I know all the girls, like I know my family; and with the members who come for their lunch, you feel that they appreciate your work, that they care for you.

Only the women working in a few of the small dining-rooms at Michael Lansby expressed feelings like these. There too, they said that they enjoyed the friendly, informal atmosphere, and that they felt people 'cared' for them. There can be no doubt that in the impersonal factories and bureaucracies of advanced capitalism, there is little room for interpersonal warmth and feeling, those qualities which Saint George's staff found and appreciated in their work.[4]

To recapitulate: for the workers at Saint George's, like for the women in the small areas at Michael Lansby, pleasant working conditions and good workmates were the two more prominent expectations towards their job. It is not surprising then that these expectations were met by their actual work situation. They generally liked working in a small place, where their relations were personal and informal, they enjoyed their working conditions and the 'atmosphere' of the club, they found their jobs interesting and took considerable pride in them. For these reasons, their dissatisfaction with pay was pushed to the background. Their work involved considerable skills in producing a highly polished product using simple technology. These skills, however, were not recognized as such and were not reflected in the workers' wages.

What of the club as a catering business? When compared to all the other catering establishments I investigated, the first impression is that Saint George's represents a lasting anachronism both in terms of the services it offers and in terms of the economics of these services. The number of staff employed seems totally out of proportion to the number of meals which they actually prepared and served – Saint George's ratio of meals prepared and served per member of staff is well under one tenth of that of any other catering establishment which I visited. In fact, I suspect that this ratio is low even by domestic cooking standards. Few businessmen would choose to run a business which employs 7 people to cater for 20-odd clients. Yet there are quite a few businessmen who would, at least occasionally, choose to have their meals at precisely this type of establishment. And this illustrates an extremely important feature of the club – as far as its members are concerned the club offers far more than a decent, traditional meal; the club offers its members a whole range of *intangible products*, a place where important contacts can be made, where guests can be offered hospitality, where information can be exchanged, where certain rituals can be preserved and daily re-enacted. The very anachronistic nature of the club is part of its appeal; it is the appeal of the old. As a time-capsule of a bygone age, it preserves in miniature all those qualities that modern industry has dissolved, qualities which linger on in memory without probably ever having existed. It is perhaps ironic that the gentlemen's club, like its diametrical opposite in catering, the fast-food store, provides its clients with an image as much as with a meal. But while the marketing wizards have carefully manufactured and disseminated the youthful, dynamic image of the fast-food industry, the gentlemen's club must rely on its natural image, tradition.

In this way, Saint George's is patronized by its members not merely as a dining-club, but as a significant part of their identity, as a stubborn refuge of constancy in a changing world. And in this context, the staff members serve much more than meals and any attempt to assess the efficiency of their work in terms of meals served per person is misleading; surely any attempt to rationalize the club's catering operation would undermine the very qualities which the club's members value. The only way of assessing the club's success is through its ability to survive precisely by providing those 'intangible' services to its members which cannot be rationalized and incorporated in catering machinery.

CHAPTER 5
The small independent restaurant or café:
The price of independence

> I regret going into catering because I am my own prisoner; I haven't had a day off or a holiday for years. I want to get rid of this place as soon as the lease runs out. Perhaps I would like to open a little restaurant, but without evening work; or perhaps a dry-cleaning shop. We have no social life now. I don't see my family enough.
>
> Suleiman Nazim,
> owner of kebab restaurant

In 1983, there were over 27,000 fish and chips shops, sandwich and snack-bars and take-away shops in this country, as well as over 12,000 restaurants and cafés providing meals on the premises. Of these, some 3,000 were Chinese, some 2,000 Indian and Pakistani, some 2,000 Italian, some 500 Greek and Turkish and some 100 French.[1] Few of these establishments are part of a larger chain, and a large majority can be regarded as independent family businesses. What is perhaps surprising is that these family businesses are often competing directly for customers with the large fast-food chains and that their numbers have actually increased since the Second World War. Unlike the grocery trade, where the rise of the supermarkets and superstores signalled the decline of the corner shop, catering has permitted independent family businesses to co-exist with outlets or franchises of large multinational firms, frequently selling the same products to the same customers.

There is such diversity in the range and quality of services which this independent sector of catering provides that an entire survey could be based on it. All I was hoping to do in the context of this research was to obtain a picture, however sketchy, of what work is like in these smaller workplaces, in which the bosses themselves do a lot of the work, often working side by side with their employees. This is the realm of the petty bourgeoisie, that class of self-employed entrepreneurs so beloved of the Conservative government of the day and so scorned by the sociologists. The number of self-employed people in Britain fell by 100,000 in the 1970s to reach 1.84 million in 1979. But this number had risen by nearly 25 per cent to 2.43 million by March 1984. In 1979, the self-employed accounted for 7.4 per cent of the labour force, while in 1984 this had risen to 10.4 per cent, which is the highest percentage on record.[2]

It is a well-documented statistical fact that self-employment is concentrated in a few sectors, such as distribution, repairs and catering (the so-called 'miscellaneous services') and the construction industry (among younger men). In 1984, nearly one in three of the self-employed worked in miscellaneous services; moreover their number has grown faster in the previous five years than any other group, apart from those in scientific and professional services. In 1984, 794,000 self-employed people worked in miscellaneous services, up from 636,000 in 1979.[3] This is reflected in the substantial increase in the number of businesses in this sector. The total number of catering businesses had increased from 109,471 in 1980 to 114,563 in 1983; in the same period, restaurants and cafés had increased from 11,512 to 12,119, while fish and chips and take-away outlets increased from 22,715 to 27,049.[4]

Contrary, then, to the expectations of some that this class of self-employed individuals would eventually 'sink into the proletariat', their numbers have swollen in recent years and catering has been one of the major areas of the economy which they have sought to colonize. As the authors of the *Market Intelligence* report on catering have argued:

> The great changes that have come about to the restaurant business in this country [since the Second World War] are largely a result of individual enterprise. Owning a restaurant is one of the well-worn routes to economic independence, especially for ethnic minorities, and though it is a route littered with failures the success rate, especially with family-run businesses, is relatively high compared with many other small businesses. (Mintel, August 1983:68)

I decided to investigate a couple of independent family establishments to get a taste of the petty bourgeois sector of catering, to study how it can compete against the heavy battalions of fast food

The small independent restaurant or café

and to examine whether owning a restaurant meets the image, described above, as a route towards economic independence. I chose two east London restaurants owned by Turkish Cypriots and run as family businesses, rarely employing staff from outside the family. After several visits, I interviewed the owners and the relatives working with them.

The first one was the Venus, a fish and chips restaurant owned and run by two brothers with the help of one full-time serving-lady and occasional part-time workers. It was conveniently located near a popular shopping and market area, drawing many of its customers from among the shoppers. The brothers had bought the restaurant a year earlier as an on-going concern, and had tried to maintain the restaurant's reputation as serving some of the best fish and chips in London. The restaurant gave the impression of a thriving business, with a constant stream of customers from noon till 7 p.m. closing time, most of whom were regulars. The largest part of its trade was take-away meals, but its fifteen-odd tables were always occupied at lunchtime. On average 400 meals were served daily, although this number rose on Fridays and Saturdays. This does not include the huge number of chips portions – about 500 lb of potatoes were fried daily.

Its success was due to a combination of skilful management and very hard work. Both owners worked on average for 80 hours per week, doing virtually all the tasks except serving at the tables and washing up; they bought the cooking materials, cut the fish, peeled and chipped the potatoes using the types of cooking instruments one uses at home. They did *all* of the cooking themselves, but spent little time on accounts, keeping only rudimentary records of their trade. They had no special interest in cooking or catering, they saw themselves as businessmen and approached their work purely as a business. This does not mean that they had no pride in their business: 'We have the best fish and chips,' said Gursel, the younger brother, an opinion clearly backed by the large number of customers who patronized their restaurant in spite of its above-average prices: 'People look for a good meal and will pay as long as the product is good.' Quality was seen as the main weapon against their competitors, other fish and chips shops in the area.

Both brothers expressed great satisfaction with their business, which they saw as a long-term investment. Erdinc, the older, said:

I am happy being a businessman, and this is a good business;

The small independent restaurant or café

> I am not planning of changing my job. I get on well with my brother and my workers, we try to understand each other. Above all, the business is making good money for us, would *you* leave such a business?

Neither brother complained about the long hours they worked; they simply regarded it as the inevitable price of success in business. As Gursel said, 'I'd work hard, whatever job I did.' Recruiting part-time staff proved quite difficult: 'Working here for 25 hours a week, they make £32 and the work is not easy. They can get £25 on the dole, just staying at home. Most of them only last for a few weeks.'

Unfortunately, I was unable to interview properly the full-time woman worker, who had been working at the restaurant for several years, since before the brothers bought it. Some of my students, however, had worked in small catering establishments, like Venus, side by side with their employers and their views are extremely interesting. Vernon had spent three summer holidays working at a fish and chips restaurant in a seaside resort. In the summer of 1985 he had earned £185 per week, putting in 80 to 100 hours of work. He was pleased with the job and planned to return to it.

> The pay was reasonable because I wasn't getting taxed. If I got taxed, then it wouldn't really be reasonable. All in all the job meets my expectations; it's a ready source of cash; it's also a challenge, because you are always looking to improve the way things are done. All meals are free and the money I earn goes straight to the bank account.

Dino, a South American student, had worked in a sandwich bar in Soho to help finance his studies; his description of his work must be characteristic of many workers working in the independent sector of catering.

> I liked the informal atmosphere [at work]. The advantages were that you laughed a lot, you talked a lot and you ate a lot. The bosses were all right, they knew how to motivate people; they used to buy drinks for the staff and made you feel that they cared for you. In return you had to work hard, nearly all the time. . . . The work wasn't pleasant. It's a dirty job, cleaning floors and toilets. It's smelly and hot, especially when you work near the ovens. And the facilities for staff and the equipment were inadequate.

The small independent restaurant or café

Hard work, continuous work, is a hallmark of this type of catering. It is possible that there is more variety than in fast food where many workers do the same thing all day long, but the work is if anything harder. Vernon:

> The pressure is always on to work quicker. If there is a queue you cannot work quickly enough in the job of providing food for the customers. If there is not a queue the pressure is still on to get ready for the next queue. There was always work, at any hour of the day. If you are not getting ready for later that day, you are catching up from yesterday or preparing for tomorrow. But unlike those working in fast food I had a lot of responsibility.

Vernon explained that he felt responsible because it was up to him to maintain the high standards of the food, to keep the equipment in good working order and to serve the customers quickly and efficiently. His description of his relation with his boss is extremely lucid, and could be used as an example of the 'simple' control identified by Richard Edwards.[5]

> Of course, my boss appreciates the pressures of my job, but he increases them to make you do things quicker. You feel that he is trying to get work from you for every penny that he pays you. Mind you, he too works hard, but you can see him thinking all the time, 'Is everyone working full out? What else could he be doing?' ... He is very working class and sees himself on par with the workers.

I suspect that many of the workers in this sector of catering would describe their bosses in a similar way. Hard work, long hours, direct control and informal relations appear to be important features of work in the independent sector of catering.

A year after my interviews with the owners, business at the Venus continued to be brisk, in spite of a sharp increase in its prices. The restaurant expanded in size, and it was redecorated, introducing new fast food style seating. The older customers had some difficulty squeezing themselves in the bright, plastic seats, but squeeze they did and the place was packed at lunchtime.

In contrast to this successful business, the owner of the second independent restaurant I visited was having considerable difficulties

The small independent restaurant or café

during this period of economic recession. Suleiman, the owner of Kismet kebab house, is an extremely articulate, sincere individual who talked to me at length about the problems of running a business of his own. Having completed a traineeship, he worked as a welder for twelve years before he decided to become his 'own boss'. Deciding to start a catering business was not difficult:

> I worked for a year at my older brother's restaurant, where I learnt the trade. Opening a restaurant seemed the obvious choice. You don't need much capital and the skills I picked them up easily. . . . I have no special interest in cooking, I never cook at home, and even here, I don't feel that I am cooking – it's just a way of doing business.

His restaurant, always spotlessly clean, had a slightly forlorn air at lunchtime, in comparison with the Venus; on several occasions, I was the only customer, as most of the trade was in take-aways. Recently, two new kebab houses had opened, directly competing with his for a limited trade. In addition the prices of his materials and rent had more than doubled in the previous couple of years. To add insult to injury VAT was imposed on take-away meals in the spring 1984 budget. Although he had managed to keep his trade at about 300 kebabs per day, this was achieved by keeping his prices as low as possible. This had meant that he had to stop employing part-time staff, relying wholly on himself, his brother and other relatives to run the restaurant.

As most of his trade was late-night take-aways, after the closing-time of pubs, Suleiman kept his restaurant open until 1 a.m. and rarely left before that. This meant that he worked a minimum of 70 hours per week, including Sundays and Saturdays, with no holidays or rest days. Nor did he find much of his work inherently pleasing; cooking was just part of doing business:

> I am a practical kind of person; car mechanics give me satisfaction or decorating this place. Time goes so quickly then, when you do something you like.

Like the owners of the Venus, Suleiman clearly saw himself as a businessman and catering as a means towards economic independence.

His younger brother, aged 18, worked much the same hours, preparing, cooking and serving meals. Unlike Suleiman, he liked cooking, and hoped to get enough experience in order to open a

The small independent restaurant or café

restaurant of his own. He was happy working for his brother and was pleased with the informal work arrangements. He felt that if he went to work late one day, or if he had to take a day off, a relative would always cover for him and this gave him a sense of freedom. Although he did not earn much, he did not mind; he had no obligations, lived at home with his parents, and his money was his own.

The business had been set up four years earlier, but running it in the present recession had become increasingly difficult. Suleiman expressed a certain anxiety about staying afloat in the face of rising prices and increasing competition. He saw the competition coming from other kebab houses rather than from the several fast-food chain stores which had recently opened in the area. Confronting these problems for him meant keeping his prices low and the quality of his meals high and he had been forced to work longer and longer hours. Unlike his brother and the owners of the fish and chips restaurant (all of whom had been on this kind of work for fewer years), he was clearly beginning to become disaffected with the long hours and described himself as 'my own prisoner':

> I hardly have any time of my own; my work follows me twenty-four hours a day, wherever I go, whatever I do. If I tried to forget about it for a while, I'd be out of business before I realized it.

For all this he wouldn't consider working 9 to 5 for somebody else. His job gave him a sense of independence and satisfaction; ultimately he felt in control of his own economic fate. Going without holidays and weekends with his family, spending 70 to 80 hours per week on hard work which he didn't find inherently pleasant, sacrificing his 'social life', these were the price he had to pay for living without bosses and supervisors, without other people's rules and regulations, without depending on others for his job and the livelihood of his family:

> I'm my own boss, no one to tell me what to do, what to say, no clocking in and out of work, no one to make me redundant.

In the last resort, Suleiman, like other small property owners, enjoys a sense of choice in his life. The forces which confront him may be formidable and beyond his control, as Marx and others recognized. However, his ultimate survival in a hostile world is perceived as depending on his own efforts, on his ability and hard work. In spite of his ambivalence about his work, he felt that his life was determined by his own actions.

> I'd never go back to a 9 to 5 job, where you're just a little cog on someone else's machine. Here, I know that I can stand or fall by my own actions; if this store doesn't work out, I can try something different, I can open a different business, I can try out something new; but I'd never go to work for someone else.

In contrast to the feelings of being trapped in their work described by other catering staff, Suleiman's feelings express an attitude to life and work which comes from the world of a different social class. For him, like for the workers of Saint Theresa's or Michael Lansby, life is neither easy nor especially pleasant. However, it is not a brutalizing experience to be endured with a laugh and a joke; it is more a course with obstacles to be overcome. To be sure these obstacles necessitate sacrifices, but they are endured in the firm belief that success lies at the end of the course.

> I dream of the day when I can retire; own several restaurants all running smoothly by themselves; give my wife and my children the kind of life we've been dreaming of; spend a lot of time with them; travel a lot; do the things that give me satisfaction, not for the money – that will have been taken care of – but for pleasure.

This vision motivates his daily efforts and justifies all the sacrifices that he has to make.

However, sacrifices he has to make; Suleiman's deep ambivalence, his pride at being his 'own boss' and his frustration at being his 'own prisoner', lies at the core of the predicament of the class which Marx called the 'petty bourgeoisie' and consistently regarded as a transitional class. There is no doubt that petty bourgeois autonomy ('being your own boss') is in a large measure an illusion, as Wright (1985:53ff) and others have shown. Competing against the vast resources of big capital, constrained by creditors and markets, relying on their ingenuity and hard work to eke out a living, many of the self-employed have precious little freedom, in deciding how they produce, what they produce or how they spend their time. Unlike many waged workers, they cannot even draw a line between work and leisure and strive to enjoy life outside work. Their work preoccupies them constantly.

However, even if autonomy is largely illusory, it is a powerful

The small independent restaurant or café

illusion, one which offers substantial satisfaction and for which many of the self-employed are prepared to toil.[6] Moreover, some of their autonomy *is* real, even if some Marxists have been unwilling to accept it. As Giddens has argued:

> If it is the case that the chances of mobility, either inter- or intragenerationally, from small to large property ownership are slight, this is likely to isolate the small property-owner from membership of the upper class as such. But the fact that he enjoys directive control of an enterprise, however minute, acts to distinguish him from those who are part of a hierarchy of authority in a larger organization. (1973:110)

At a time when large areas of catering are appropriated by the big fast-food battalions with massive purchasing power, with scientific planning and administration, using the latest technologies of cooking, preserving and serving meals and mobilizing all the skills of the image-makers, the survival and success of independent catering establishments reflects the ingenuity and extraordinary motivation of those who run them. How else would it be possible for these obstinate catering Davids to compete against the international Goliaths of the trade, frequently undercutting their prices and matching their much-vaunted quality? While unable to compete with the fast-food chains in terms of technical and administrative efficiency, the independents must outperform them in terms of human efficiency. I estimated that in each of the two restaurants I visited 100 meals are served per worker each day, a truly prodigious figure, when one takes into account the limited use of ready or convenience foods sold. The kebabs are made using fresh meat, the fish is bought fresh and then boned, cut and seasoned. Potatoes are bought fresh in bags of 60 lb, peeled, chipped and fried on the premises, using rudimentary machinery and a lot of hard work. By comparison, the use of labour by the big fast-food chains seems hopelessly inefficient.

In these smaller catering establishments labour emerges with crystal clarity as the indispensable ingredient for profits and indeed for economic survival. Unlike the world of mega-capital where profits 'appear' to result from the efforts of technocrats, marketers and planners, in the world of the small fry it is labour, hard, ingenious, impromptu and continuous, which ultimately makes the difference between survival and bankruptcy. Of course, markets, customers, competitors, creditors have all a part in deciding the success or failure of the business. But labour is the one factor over which the small entrepreneur has some control; and it is labour that the small entrepreneur contributes liberally, and it is labour that he expects from workers and family.

My discussions with the owners of these two restaurants and the relatives who worked for them leaves no doubt that their tremendous motivation is the result of the great value attached to economic independence. 'I like being my own boss with no one to tell me what to do,' I was told again and again. Economic independence, for its part, is the basis of a more general feeling of freedom, self-sufficiency and self-determination.

And here lies the paradox: for it is this very economic independence that poses more serious restrictions on the self-employed restaurateur's private and family life than any boss would ever be allowed to make. Children's labour legislation, health and safety legislation, statutory holidays and the like do not apply in such small family businesses, where every sacrifice has to be made in order to keep the business going. It is only by appreciating the magnitude and the extent of this sacrifice that one can appreciate how important economic independence is for these individuals.

CHAPTER 6
Conclusions: Keeping the lid on

Long before the droves of bleary-eyed commuters begin to rub shoulders on their way to another day in the office, an army of people is at work. They are busily cleaning up offices, preparing breakfasts, stocking up store shelves, vacuuming hotel lobbies, sweeping airport corridors, emptying brimming dustbins, manning petrol stations. Many of them will still be working long after the offices have emptied and their occupants are slumped in front of television sets, dreaming of summer holidays or planning the evening's entertainment. Few of the millions working in the so-called twilight trades enjoy the comforts of 9 to 5; few spend their weekends recovering and relaxing.[1]

By 8 a.m., Maria Romano has been punching the keys of her cash register for an hour, as nurses, midwives, ancillaries and visitors are having breakfast in the round-the-clock dining-room of Saint Theresa's; Suarez and his fellow porters have already carted their trolleys with breakfasts to the wards; the pile of washing up for Juan is several feet high. A few miles away, Thérèse, the young French woman who stayed in London after joining a religious group, is serving breakfast at a West End hotel before she starts grilling hamburgers at Fun Food. At the Fun Food flagship outlet Nick, Robert, Firoz and the other managers on shift are planning their day, checking their inventories and making sure that they will have enough staff to cope with the onslaught of customers at the peak times. Eric and Sharon are already serving muffins, eggs and bacon in bright red packages; the rush is not on yet, just the odd customer at the end of his shift on his way home.

Fifteen hours later many of these people are still working or are on their way home. The pubs have just closed and in the next hour or two Suleiman at the Kismet kebab house will be selling more kebabs than he did during the previous twelve hours. Yvonne, the black supervisor at Fun Food 3, is on her way home after a twelve-hour shift, while Andy will be clearing up and taking stock; he is hoping to finish by 2 a.m. and have a few hours sleep before the managers start to arrive at 6 a.m.; he will be dreaming of his future career in the RAF.

The aim of this book was to present an accurate picture of the working lives and outlooks of some of these people, who, while working around the clock, have become invisible to virtually everyone, the media, trade unions, politicians, academic researchers and even the public they serve. As Sharon said in the Preface:

> You serve hundreds of people here each day. Some of them are regular, I see them every Saturday. But most of them hardly seem to notice you – all they want is to get served as soon as possible and that's all that matters. Sometimes I think that this uniform makes me invisible.

In addition, I studied catering as an area where rich profits are being made through the application of mass production techniques imported from manufacturing. Finally, the book is an account of workplace relations in Britain in the 1980s, when capital in the persons of Edwardes, McGregor, Murdoch and others has challenged the traditions of management by consent and collective bargaining and has sought to re-assert its 'right to manage'.

Catering workers work in an industry of bewildering variety and complexity. They work in different work environments doing very different types of work. They produce a vast array of products and services, employing diverse techniques and equipment. They come from different backgrounds and bring to their work a large variety of outlooks and expectations. The 175 or so workers and managers whose experiences are at the centre of this book are part of the human backbone of catering. Saint Theresa's, with its large number of older immigrant workers who felt trapped in dead-end jobs due to their poor command of the language, age and general insecurity, and also the younger group of qualified, skilled cooks who regarded their stint with the NHS as a stepping stone for better things. Michael Lansby, with a workforce made up almost exclusively of married women with children at school, whose repetitive work offered few intrinsic pleasures, but a strong feeling of solidarity and togetherness. Fun Food, with its teenage workforce who approached their work as a brief interlude to be 'lasted out' for as long as the economic rewards outweighed the tedium and pressure of the job.

Conclusions

Saint George's, with its small workforce for whom the intimate and informal atmosphere of the club compensated for the poor pay. And the small independent fish and chips and kebab owners, for whom long work-hours and arduous work were seen as the price of independence.

The economic and political environment

In spite of this variety, the single factor which was actively felt in every establishment was the present social and economic depression and the government's handling of it. In every establishment, the realities of the workplace were intricately connected with the economic and political realities of the time. The field research took place in 1984, when mass unemployment already dominated British society. With one out of seven workers officially unemployed, the dole was a daily reality for the millions out of work and a constant threat for many of the rest. Unemployment among the young was at least twice as high. Union membership was in rapid decline; unions had lost over 2 million members in five years, and for the first time in years spoke for less than half of the country's workers.

A Conservative government, in the aftermath of its Falklands triumph, was confronted by a split opposition in Parliament. The Labour party, after a disastrous electoral defeat in 1983, was trying to patch up its internal divisions under a new leadership. Organized labour was everywhere on the defensive. A subtle and piecemeal legislative assault on the powers of unions was complemented by a succession of industrial defeats inflicted on them. One after another labour battalion succumbed – dockers, shipbuilding workers, steel workers, British Leyland workers, railways workers had all experienced bitter and humiliating defeats.

The major political event of the period of my research was the beginning of the miners' strike which led to the most bitter and decisive of all the defeats. The strike, punctuated by brutal confrontations between striking miners and police as well as by violent incidents against non-strikers, deeply polarized the country and the labour movement. The strike epitomized the confrontation between the government's economic philosophy of the survival of the economically fit and traditional working-class values of community, solidarity and the fight for jobs. Its outcome marked the decisive shift

Conclusions

in the balance of power in management's favour and the increasing powerlessness of organized labour in a period of economic slump.

The same shift was evident in another significant event of the period, the government's off-hand banning of unions at the headquarters of intelligence services at Cheltenham, after the unions had already given a no-strike undertaking. This was interpreted by many as the final proof that the only good trade union, for the government, was a dead one.[2] The unions, it was implied, had not merely brought the country to the brink of economic collapse in pursuit of their petty sectarian pursuits; narrow self-interest also made them a threat to national security. In the aftermath of the Falklands, the patriotism of unionists was called into question and in an unprecedented gesture the government offered to each unionist at GCHQ £1000 in exchange for surrendering their statutory rights and their union cards.

This, then, was the backcloth of my research – some called it economic realism, others were less polite. Most of the managers I interviewed talked with enthusiasm about the new outlook which had finally prevailed over their staff, moderating their demands and disciplining their behaviour. Mr Gorman, a top catering manager in the National Health Service, said:

> There is a new realism now among the staff. They realize that the days when the budget was automatically topped up are gone. They also realize that unless they do an honest day's work their jobs will disappear. Their expectations have finally come down to earth and they are willing to co-operate with us.

Mike Robins, the union Branch Secretary at the same hospital, expressed things differently, but the message is the same:

> They are afraid to talk, they are afraid to complain. They are afraid for their jobs, they are afraid for their future. Of course, management have taken full advantage of this fear to reassert their control.

Fear, or what managers called with ritual regularity 'new realism', was the great common denominator in the lives of most workers in this book. This was the major unifying factor in their experiences at the workplace. It affected every attitude and coloured every sentiment of the workers everywhere; it depressed expectations, undermined opposition to management and inhibited solidarity. This fear was sometimes explicit, sometimes implicit, but its importance is hard to over-estimate. Yet most industrial sociologists have overlooked it, by isolating the workplace from the broader social and economic realities which surround it. For the workers whose working lives are the heart of this book, the broader social and economic realities were a feature of their everyday work reality.

Blackwell and Seabrook (1985), in a provocative discussion, have argued that far from being characteristics of periods of economic depression fear and insecurity are part and parcel of the historical experience of the British working class. Generations of British workers have lived with insecurity – that their skills will be dispossessed, that they will fall victim to accident, to technical rationalization or to their employers' whim, that their neighbourhoods will be taken over for redevelopment, that their children will end up in the borstal. This is the insecurity of those whose fates are permanently decided by others.

> It is perhaps the uncertainty and unpredictability of working class experience, its very driven quality, which has produced such a strong vein of conservatism in working class life. Although this working class conservatism has often been misunderstood, even denied, or denounced as false consciousness, its roots are not hard to find. For not only does it represent a perfectly rational response in that it seeks to appease those whose wealth and power are the main determinants of working class life chances; it also reflects a deep desire to cling to the remnants of those defences which generations of working class energies have constructed against the most violent inroads of capitalism. (1985:35)

Working in the 'new' service sector, the workers whose stories are described in this book do not meet the traditional proletarian stereotype. Yet, their stories are part of the same historical experience. Insecurity and fear dominated their outlooks, with the prospect of unemployment never far from their minds. Some responded with resigned pessimism and suppressed anger, some with cheerful defiance. Protecting their job was their primary pre-occupation. Within such a context, traditional theories of worker motivation seeking to encourage hard work through extrinsic and intrinsic rewards appear quite irrelevant, as many of the managers told me. 'The novelty and fun of fast food may be a motivator to begin with; but those who stay here stay because they need the money; ... no other motivation is necessary these days.' Needing the money means needing the job – this is the simple equation which dominated the outlook of the clear majority of workers in this book.

It is naive to regard workers who are tied to their jobs by economic need as 'economic men', after the Taylorist stereotype, concerned only to maximize their pay packet. To describe workers on £57 net per week as money-grabbers, as did one of Saint Theresa's managers, defies credibility. It also clashes with the workers' own attitudes towards work. Although most workers depended on their job for their livelihood, not a single group in my sample saw good pay as the most desirable quality of a good job. Interest and variety was seen as more desirable than good pay by all groups except for the ancillary workers at Saint Theresa's, for whom job security and good workmates were most important. Those who said that they stayed in their job because they needed the money said so because their jobs had little else to offer, not because they approached work purely as a means towards earning money.

'Trapped in a job'

Far from having an instrumental orientation and choosing jobs which maximized economic rewards, most of the workers in my sample had an instrumental orientation *thrust upon them* by unrewarding jobs and lack of alternatives due to the economic slump. Although several 'kept their eyes open' for alternative employment, few of the workers in my sample had systematically set out to investigate whether there were other jobs available. Age, lack of qualifications and training, poor command of the language, the chores of housekeeping and the need to look after children outside school hours, all compounded the feeling that 'there is no alternative'.

'There Is No Alternative' (as well as the other celebrated slogan of the 1980s, 'On Your Bike') is not just the catchphrase in the new Conservative political vocabulary. It has also become part of the vocabulary of everyday workplace experience. As a political slogan, 'There Is No Alternative' presents Margaret Thatcher's unrestrained capitalism as the only answer to Britain's economic ills. As a daily reality it expresses the workers' insecure claustrophobia, the feeling of being trapped in jobs which they desperately need but which are for much of the time unbearable. Neither the immediate work reality nor the broader political reality allows the workers

Conclusions

much room for movement, discussion or negotiation. Not much freedom of choice for them.

It is hardly surprising, then, that a majority of the workers I interviewed felt trapped in their jobs. For most of them the notion of choice was incomprehensible. Mrs Jean Harrison, 54, had cooked at Michael Lansby for ten years; her disabled husband did not work and three of her six children still lived at home:

> At my age, with no special skills, with a family to take care of, there is no other job I could do; sure, I used to look at the paper for other jobs, but then I gave up. There just isn't anything. So, I cling on to this one until I retire, what else can I do?

Jose-Luis Suarez, the trolley-porter at Saint Theresa's:

> We just hang on and hang on. What else is there to do? I will end my days as a worker here, either for retirement or for the dole. Everyday I come here and I feel depressed; after fifteen years of working here and I still don't know if there will be a job for me next week or not.

Such views, expressing a lifetime's experiences of being denied the dignity of work ('respect' was the word Suarez used), are a world apart from the confident, outward-oriented world of the middle class, typified by many of the managers and the self-employed caterers in this book. For them, life, in spite of all its adversities, could be controlled and dominated through activity and free choice.

The only other groups who felt that they were in control of their lives, choosing from among different alternatives, were the younger workers at Saint Theresa's and Fun Food. Free of family burdens, unlike the older workers, they had not yet experienced the crippling effect of doing an unrewarding job *and at the same time of depending on such a job*. It is not accidental that these younger workers were also the only workers who generally did not express direct fears of unemployment. Many of their friends outside work were on the dole, and unemployment for them was not associated either with poverty and destitution or with stigma and social exclusion. The scarcity of jobs did, however, moderate their expectations and made them accept what they regarded as unrewarding work: 'A job is better than no job, for the time being at least. It keeps me busy; I was so bored at home. Also the people you meet here. But when they [managers] get on my nerves, I think I won't come to the job the next day,' said one of the Fun Food supervisors, who added that when people asked her where she worked she told them: 'At a smelly old burger joint.' Comments like these show that the expectations of many of the younger workers were lowered by an awareness that 'a job is better than no job'; this makes virtually any job acceptable – at least until it becomes unbearable.

Pay

For most of the catering workers in this book there was no question of a choice between well-paid intrinsically unpleasant jobs and more intrinsically rewarding but less-well-paid ones; their jobs were generally seen as both intrinsically unrewarding *and* badly paid ones. At a time when average hourly pay for full-time male workers stood at £3.19, virtually all workers in my sample received less than £2.00 per hour; even when overtime and shiftwork are taken into account, very few took home more than £100 per week, confirming the position of catering as being at the bottom of the wages league. Moreover, many of these workers were among the worst-paid employees *within* the catering industry, where earnings for full-time males averaged £2.64.

Catering jobs pay badly. This study, however, does not support the view that low pay is the factor which causes *most* dissatisfaction at work. Nor does low pay have the same implications for all catering workers. Unmarried teenagers, living at home with their families with few obligations and little previous work experience, are less concerned about the level of pay than some of the cook-freeze staff supporting a family and an unemployed husband or some of the hospital porters trying to make ends meet in expensive London. For them travel alone absorbed 10 per cent of their net earnings and a daily meal in the hospital canteen a further 5 to 10 per cent.

In spite of these different implications of low pay, the findings flatly contradict the common assumption that women, especially in low-paid, part-time jobs, work on the whole for pin money. Only 2 of the 111 women in my sample agreed with this view; for the remaining 109 the money they earned was either an indispensable part of the family budget or, for the younger ones living with their parents, a source of independence and a means of fulfilling their needs. While, therefore, money was not the most highly valued

Conclusions

attribute of work and the overall level of pay was low, it was the factor which kept these women in what were generally regarded as undesirable jobs, in cook-freeze kitchen and fast food, in hospital catering and school-meals.

It is very telling that in spite of the extremely low level of wages, only 20 out of 143 manual workers in my sample regarded poor pay as the main problem with their work. Thirty-seven manual workers saw management or supervision as the major problem with their job and 45 said that the work itself caused most unhappiness. Given a choice, it is likely that a far greater number would have moved to a more interesting job or a job with better supervision than to a better paid one, for in the last resort it is not bad pay but dehumanizing work and contemptuous treatment which inflicted on the workers the sense of injured dignity and powerlessness.

Job satisfaction

Only three groups of the workers found their work intrinsically satisfying or challenging, the hospital cooks, the staff serving in small dining areas at Michael Lansby and the staff in the gentlemen's club. Freedom from interference was a feature of the work situation of all of these groups. The hospital cooks experienced considerable autonomy at work and freedom to use their skills and abilities in producing a product which gave them a sense of pride. Some of them had a 'craft orientation' towards their work and their frustrations resulted from an inability to reach the highest standards of cooking while working for the NHS. Most of them were committed to a career in catering and hoped to move to more rewarding jobs or restaurant ownership, once they had served their apprenticeships in hospital catering. Catering assistants in the smaller areas of Michael Lansby did not have a craft orientation; they did, however, experience a freedom from interference and direct supervision, which allowed them to socialize with the customers and control their work environment to a degree. Finally, the staff at Saint George's Club enjoyed its genial and informal atmosphere and most of them felt happy in their work, in spite of the low level of pay. They felt that their work was appreciated and that they were respected and valued as individuals by the club's members.

The self-employed owners of the fish and chips and kebab

restaurants reported a considerable degree of job satisfaction; this, however, was not the result of the intrinsic aspects of the work, which they found unrewarding. What they did enjoy was the feeling of independence, of being responsible for themselves. They considered themselves businessmen, not caterers, and would move to another business if they could make a success of it.

All but 4 of the 27 managers and clerical workers I interviewed reported a high level of job satisfaction; many of them described their work as a challenge and the vast majority approached it as a career. Only one of them expressed profound depression about his work, similar to that reported by many of the workers at Saint Theresa's and Michael Lansby. Although several complained about the ignorance of their superiors (especially those at Michael Lansby, who had no end of complaints against their municipal administrators) or about the long hours of work, they generally identified with their employer and appeared to do their utmost to serve their employer's interests.

For a substantial majority of the workers the question of job satisfaction never arose. Work was to be endured not enjoyed. As Vassilis Pappas, one of the older porters at Saint Theresa's, said:

> The only enjoyment I get in this job is when it's time to go home, especially if I have two [rest] days to spend at home with my wife and children. When I'm here I'm just surviving; and in order to survive you have to share a joke and keep yourself out of the way of management.

Different groups of workers developed different survival tactics, but, with the exception of some of the foreign workers at Saint Theresa's who felt isolated and kept themselves to themselves, the majority sought comfort in comradeship with their mates. Daydreaming, joking or fantasizing were all important in this context but perhaps the most significant was an ongoing attempt to put their own stamp, however small or symbolic, on their work.

Technology is of considerable importance here. As a force moulding the nature of jobs, it affects the levels and types of skills, the degree of control workers can exercise over their jobs, the variety and quality of the work itself. Simple cooking technologies allow cooks a virtually free hand to produce a product which reflects their skill and imagination. If you take six competent cooks, give them the same ingredients, equipment and recipes and ask them to prepare the same dish, you are likely to end with six different dishes,

Conclusions

each reflecting the qualities, skills and tastes of the person who cooked it. Some catering technologies allow the worker some scope to affect only the speed of production, the quality of the product or its presentation. Some, however, have been devised with the expressed intention to remove the human factor from catering, to 'stop cooks messing about with the recipes'. In order to assess the degree to which technology affects the quality of jobs and the workers' satisfaction, an index was compiled measuring the quality of different catering jobs and the amount of autonomy experienced by each individual – the higher an individual's score on the index the greater the amount of control he/she enjoyed in their job and the better the overall quality of the job.[3]

Table 6.1 indicates that groups with higher Job Index scores reported higher overall job satisfaction. Management, hospital cooks, fast-food supervisors and the staff at Saint George's Club

TABLE 6.1
Job Index Scores and Job Satisfaction of all groups

	Job Index	Percent who found their job 'pretty good' or better	N
All management, clerical and self-employed	20.4	71	31
Saint Theresa's			
Cooks	18.6	79	19
Kitchen-porters	16.2	20	10
Trolley-porters	13.0	28	7
Dining-room staff	14.6	35	17
Michael Lansby			
Cook-freeze cooks	14.3	24	17
Porters	14.0	33	3
FE dining staff	13.1	47	15
School-meals staff	14.2	50	8
Minor dining areas staff	14.7	67	9
Fun Food			
Supervisors	18.3	57	7
Staff	15.6	27	26
Saint George's Club			
All staff	18.3	67	6

Note: Job Index scores ranged from a possible minimum of 9 to a possible maximum of 27.

scored high on the Job Index and were generally more satisfied than cook-freeze and fast-food staff, who scored much less on the Job Index. The two groups of workers who worked with antiquated catering technologies, hospital cooks and gentlemen's club staff, were generally satisfied with their work, while cook-freeze and fast-food workers, working with the last word in catering technology, were not.[4]

While technology did have an important effect on job satisfaction, its effect was not uniform but *varied* from workplace to workplace and from one group of workers to another. Hospital cooks enjoyed their work in part at least because of a technology which allowed them scope for autonomy and creativity. For other groups, like most dining-room assistants, technology only had a peripheral significance and their work experience was primarily shaped by other factors, such as relations with managers, supervision, work-hours and workmates. In groups like cook-freeze staff and fast-food workers, advanced technology had a powerful negative effect.

Within these groups, however, it was not the case that every single individual felt equally dissatisfied; in both groups, the individuals for whom interest and variety were an important priority at work were significantly less satisfied than those with other expectations. There is no iron law stipulating that technology 'determines' the worker's experience at work or that it 'causes' worker alienation. Expectations and orientations influence individuals' responses to 'alienating' technology. But it is not just that technology does not dictate work *experience*; more importantly, it seems to me that it does not even dictate the *work itself*. Even in fast food, where it unquestionably represents an overpowering influence, I discovered considerable differences among the three Fun Food stores, which indicate that it leaves some room for manoeuvre to both management and workers. Technology does not have the last word on how much people talk to each other, nor does it dictate the degree of formality in interpersonal relations, the quality of the product, or even the speed of work. Workers will try to discover 'short-cuts', they will try to do even the simplest things 'their own way' as if they obtain a satisfaction by defying the book. In all the establishments I visited the workers tried actively to influence their work environment, to stamp their own identity on it and humanize it. A milk bottle with a couple of flowers, a transistor radio blaring at all times, a painting on the wall done by 'one of the lads', these were attempts to influence the work environment.

Conclusions

For these reasons, it is more accurate to regard technology as one of the strategic parameters within which the power game between management and workers takes place. It is part of the terrain contested daily through negotiation and confrontation, rather than just a weapon in the arsenal of management.

Workplace politics

Workplace politics do not merely reflect the class divisions of society but are an important barometer of class politics. In the 1980s, class and workplace politics have come closer still. A new breed of hard managers has emerged, who model themselves on Mr Michael Edwardes or Mr Ian McGregor and seek to re-affirm management's right to manage. 'On your bike' expresses laconically management's new-found confidence, its 'take it or leave it' attitude. Many of these new managers feel contempt for their predecessors' politics of appeasement and blame them for the unions' crippling power on the shopfloor. Whatever their rhetoric, their industrial relations is based on confrontation rather than negotiation, and they are quite willing to tolerate massive costs in pursuit of victory.

Events at Saint Theresa's and Michael Lansby are in line with such a view. In both organizations, managers had made conscious decisions to roll back the frontiers of control and reclaim lost ground, even if this required confrontation. Mr Gorman, the senior catering officer at Saint Theresa's:

> My predecessor was a nice, very compassionate man, but lacked authority; the union used to run the department. . . . We inherited a chaotic situation when we took over here. The union was, I wouldn't say destructive, but very militant. We had to take them on to introduce the new rostering system and the other changes. We've now restored discipline and control.

In a similar way, Bill Good, the catering manager at Michael Lansby, described one of his predecessors as willing to be a mere 'figurehead'; in spite of his professed human relations views, he opted for confronting his workforce in order to enforce a reduction of working hours and dissolve lines of demarcation. After an unsuccessful strike, the workers returned to work on his terms. He described the strike as 'the big storm which cleared the air' and added that the workers 'now accept what we say; they are very cooperative'. The policy of confrontation at both these catering organizations which involved strikes and other industrial action are consistent with Purcell's view that 'a new industrial relations, harsher, tougher, no-nonsense-style, is emerging: *We* manage, you, the unions, react as you always have but now the balance of power has turned in our favour' (1982:3). Aware that the balance of power in workplace politics has shifted in their favour, many managers have tried and largely succeeded in strengthening their control over their workers and increasing discipline.

In none of the establishments I investigated were the unions involved in any meaningful dialogue or negotiation with management. At Fun Food and the smaller establishments there were no unions at all; at Saint Theresa's the union had been defeated, its shrinking membership had been divided and was only just beginning to re-build some solidarity; at Michael Lansby the union only existed on paper to collect the workers' dues but was never seen on the shopfloor. In all the larger catering organizations, management sought to emulate their illustrious counterparts in the mining and motor industry by 'talking direct' to their workforce. Few of the workers had any illusions about the purpose of this communication; only a handful out of 137 workers in these larger organizations reported that there was real consultation, while several said that they were 'the last ones to know' managers' important decisions. Much of the time, the workers worried about important decisions being taken behind their back – new technology, new manning levels, new working hours, new products, new regulations, new work quotas, these were all decided in far-away places by people who approached them as figures to be juggled in accounting spreadsheets. At the end of these almost Kafkaesque deliberations, a notice on a bulletin board or a mimeographed circular and 'Take it or . . . on your bike'.

Heartened by the substantial decline in strike statistics, some have argued that a few years of the politics of shopfloor confrontation have achieved what many years of appeasement had failed to deliver – a working class which has finally understood the rules of capitalism and is willing to act its part. This is inaccurate, if the experience of catering workers in this book is anything to go by. Far from bringing workers and management closer together, the politics of confrontation have deepened the divide. Fear and defeat have undoubtedly curbed the workers' militance and have lowered their expectations; but to argue that the workers have accepted their position as supporting cast in the capitalist show and were acting their part would be very short-sighted. In spite of coming from some of the most vulnerable and exploited sections of the working class, the workers in this survey questioned at each turn management's right to manage and their obligation to obey and found different ways of establishing a measure of control over their work and their environment. And managers had to remain constantly vigilant and prepared to deal with crises and problems. Keeping the lid on their workers' discontents best describes the task facing them. Far from dissolving shopfloor politics in a well-oiled mechanism of production, in which each worker is a reliable cog, the new tough managements had merely exploited the prevailing economic conditions to modify the issues being bargained over and the method of bargaining. The new policy of industrial confrontation is but a continuation of workplace politics, only by other means.

In all the establishments described in this book, workplace politics, like the outlooks of individuals, were crucially moulded by the social and political realities of the time. It is not true, however, that workplace politics were everywhere the same. The messy and bitter politics of Saint Theresa's are a world apart from the superficially smooth operation of Michael Lansby, the rule-dominated stage of Fun Food or the interpersonal bargaining of the smaller units. These differences result from the fundamentally different types of *management control* in each organization.

At Saint Theresa's, where many of the workers (especially the cooks) exercised some craft control over their work and where the work process had never been properly planned or rationalized, management relied on direct, personal supervision to ensure overall control over the work process. As Edwards, Burawoy and others have shown, despotism and arbitrariness are crucial features of this type of control, seeking to keep the workers forever divided through unequal treatment. The allocation of overtime, promotion and other privileges, the turning of a blind eye and the strict enforcement of rules, the distribution of 'gravy jobs' and 'stinkers', of praise and reprimand, were all used extensively by management to reward those who submitted to their authority and to discipline those classed as bolshie.

By contrast, management at Michael Lansby did relatively little direct supervision and relied on the catering technology and its designers to deliver the goods. The cooks, working in conveyor-type cooking lines, submitted themselves to the technology and consistently met the quotas in order to 'keep the bosses off their backs'. In this way, they achieved a measure of control over their work environment (and to a much lesser extent over the work itself) and developed strong ties of support and solidarity among themselves.

Technology is also a key to management control in fast food, but there it was complemented by myriads of specific bureaucratic rules which governed every aspect of work. Even in fast food, however, many of the rules were habitually bent or broken, in an attempt to increase production during peak hours; management frequently turned a blind eye to such practices and this gave a measure of autonomy to the workers in their job. In the smaller units, control was personal and *ad hoc*, constantly being negotiated by harassed bosses and their few overworked employees.

In all the establishments, although the system of control varied, control over the work process was part of the terrain being contested by management and workers. And this contest for control was a central feature of workplace politics which exercised such a powerful influence on the workers' and managers' experience at the workplace. It is the realities of shopfloor politics, the day-to-day political drama and the memories of past events, battles won and lost, compromises, injustices and 'traumata' which shape the workers' and the managers' attitudes towards each other and towards their jobs.

Discontents at work

This book has focused on a small segment of the working class, working in the service industries. On the basis of their experiences at work, it would be absurd to argue that the class distinctions of society are being blurred or obliterated by the arrival of a service economy or by the onslaught of mass unemployment. I would also dispute the view that the workers have lost their ability or will to resist, fight and contest the power of capital. While the workers whose views were described here come from some of the most vulnerable and exploited sections of the working class – foreign, part-time, female, teenage, unskilled – and while their position is aggravated by economic collapse, their discontents mirror the

Conclusions

hidden injuries of class of many generations of workers who have reluctantly sold their labour power to capital. Their lot is boring work, poor working conditions, arrogant management, and above all, lack of control over those forces which dominate their lives. Like generations of workers before them, they experience deep ambivalence, depending on capital for their livelihood, feeling impotent in the face of capital and yet fighting back in significant ways.

In different establishments, the workers' discontents took different forms, commensurate with the types of control exercised by management and their specific social and economic predicament. Foreign workers at Saint Theresa's, bitter and disillusioned, trapped in their jobs by their age, lack of skill and difficulty with English, resorted to absenteeism, while the younger workers at Fun Food, still free of family commitments, just quit as soon as they had had enough. The women working at Michael Lansby, faced with the dual burdens of work inside and outside the home, tried to make do with a laugh and a joke at the bosses' expense. At the time of this study, the workers' discontents, their injured dignity, were seldom expressed in militant collective action (although they had been on earlier occasions). More often they led to individual gestures of defiance, to absenteeism, to high labour turnover and to a constant effort to grapple some control over their job and their work environment. A lot of the time these discontents were silent, just underneath the surface, behind the kitchen walls, out of the sanitized customers' sight.

If, however, most of these catering workers swallow their discontents and recognize their limited power, they have few illusions. As their words in the pages of this book testify, they understand very well what is happening and can talk about it to all who will listen. The majority are trying to make the best of a bad job. The question is whether the different sectors of catering, the service industries or capitalism can continue to accommodate the discontents they generate.

APPENDIX
The Interview Schedule

1 When did you first come to work here?
  How did you hear of this job?
2 Have you ever worked anywhere else?
3 What was the last job you did before coming here?
  (a) Type of firm or organization:
  (b) Type of job:
  (c) Length of service:
4 What were your main jobs before that?
5 Have you spent any periods of time unemployed?
6 What was your first job in this organization?
7 How long have you been in this job?
8 What exactly is your present job? How would you describe it in your own words?
9 When someone asks you what you do for a living, how do you answer?
10 What are your hours of work? How much overtime do you do on average?
11 What is your weekly pay [monthly salary]? What do you normally take home?
12 Would you describe your job as
  very skilled/skilled/semi-skilled/unskilled?
13 What training was required for this job? Have you had any training since you came here?
14 Have you had any other training or qualifications?
15 What keeps you in this job? What are the main advantages of your job?
16 What are the main problems of your work?
17 Have you ever thought of leaving this job? (Like looking for a job in the paper?) Why?
18 Would you move out of catering?
19 Here are some things often thought important about a job; which would you look for first in a job? And which next?
  Interest and variety
  Good pay and chances of overtime
  A supervisor who doesn't breathe down your neck
  Pleasant working conditions
  Good workmates

Appendix

        Helping other people
        A sense of pride and achievement in the product
        A career in catering
        Job security
        Other

20 So far as these two things are concerned would you say that your job is
    first rate/pretty good/about average/not too good/very bad?
21 What is your job security? Do you feel
    Very safe/fairly safe/rather unsafe/very insecure
22 Has the present recession affected your working conditions? How?
23 Now, I would like to ask you some more detailed questions about your job; first, do you find that you do the same things day in day out, or is every day different?
24 Do you find that you have to work too fast most of the time?
25 Does your job leave you tired at the end of the day?
26 Is it too simple to bring out your best qualities?
27 Does it give you a chance to try out your own ideas?
28 Can you do the work on the job and keep your mind on other things most of the time?
29 Is your job essential for the success of this organization?
30 Does the standard of the meals which you provide depend on how well you do your job?
31 Does your job lead to promotion if you do it well?
32 Are there any short-cuts that you can pick up to make your job easier?
33 Which one of these statements comes closer to describing how you feel about your job?
    (a) My job is interesting nearly all the time.
    (b) My job is interesting most of the time but there are some dull stretches now and then.
    (c) There are few times when my job is interesting but most of the time it is pretty dull and monotonous.
    (d) My job is completely dull and monotonous.
34 (a) Are machines your friends or your enemies in this job?
34 (b) Most of the time do you control the machines or do the machines control you?
35 Has any new technology been introduced while you have been here? New machines? New products? New systems of work?
36 Have they redesigned your job in a little or big way?
37 Has there been any rationalization to increase efficiency?

If yes
38 (a) How have these changes affected your work situation?
    (i) Have they made your job more interesting?
    (ii) Have they affected the level of skill needed by your job?
    (iii) Have they led to redundancies?
    (iv) Have they required re-training?
    (v) Have they affected your working conditions?

(vi) Do you think that workers have more responsibility since these changes? More or less control over their work?

If no
38 (b) Is it likely that any significant changes will be made in the foreseeable future? [If yes, repeat questions 38a (i) to 38a (vi) 'Would these changes ....?']
39 How is the teamwork, the co-operation among people doing different jobs here?
40 Do you prefer to work in a group or by yourself?
41 In your work how much do you talk to your workmates?
   A good deal/Just now and then/Hardly at all
42 Do you talk mainly about work or about things outside the workplace?
43 Have you made any friends since you came to work here?
44 Do you ever see your friends from work outside the workplace?
45 How would you feel about moving to a similar job but away from the people who you work with? Would you feel
   Very upset/Fairly upset/Not much bothered/Not bothered at all
46 Would you describe your direct supervisor/manager as
   friendly and informal
   formal and impersonal
   correct but unfriendly
   pushy and bossy
   other
47 Does he/she appreciate the pressures of your job?
48 Would you say that managers in this organization/department are doing a good job (i) running this department, (ii) for their staff?
49 Do they take care of their staff?
50 Would you say that they are arrogant to their staff?
51 Is there much consultation between workers and management before important decisions?
52 Are you a member of a trade union?

If yes
53 Which trade union?
54 Does your union operate a closed-shop? [If yes: Would you belong to the union if you had a choice?]
55 Would you describe yourself as a committed trade-unionist?
56 Is your union doing a good job for its members?
57 In what way?
58 How could your union improve the service it offers its members?

If no
59 Why not? [If because there is no union: Would you choose to belong to a union if there was one representing workers in this department/organization?]
60 Do you strongly agree, agree, disagree or strongly disagree with each of the following statements?
   (a) We need union protection.

Appendix

     (b) We need union help over pay and conditions.
     (c) Unions should try and get workers a say in management.
61 How would you assess the quality of the meals which are prepared here?
62 Are they good value for money?
63 Do they provide good nutrition?
64 In what ways could the service/food be improved?
65 Would you say that the people who eat these meals are satisfied or dissatisfied?
66 Would you choose to have these meals at home with your family?
67 Now, I would like to ask you some questions about your own eating habits and those of your family. Are you married? Do you have children? Who makes up your household? Is/are your husband/wife/parents employed?
68 Who decides what you eat at home? Who buys the food?
69 Who does the cooking at home?
70 Do you enjoy cooking?
     Very much/quite a lot/not so much/not at all
71 Do you get recipes from cookery books?
72 How many meals do you have each day and what do you normally eat in each meal?
73 How many hot meals did you cook last week at home?
74 How many times did you have meat or chicken last week at home?
75 Did you have any take-away meals such as sandwiches, fish and chips or hamburgers last week?
76 Did you have a meal or a snack at a pub or a restaurant?
77 Do you usually have a Sunday joint or do you prefer a different type of meal? What?
78 Going back to your work prospects, how do you see your future? What would you like to be doing in five years time?
79 Do you have any long-term plans?
80 In an ideal world what work would you like to do?
81 Do your attitudes towards your work and your employer change a lot depending on the ups and downs of the job?
82 Have your attitudes towards your work and your employer changed substantially in the last few years?
83 If had I asked the same questions on another day, might you have answered differently?
84 Are there any comments you would like to make or any questions you would like to ask?
85 All in all then, what would you say are the main advantages of your job? And the main disadvantages?

Notes

Introduction

1 There is no up-to-date authoritative data on the number of people employed in catering. Such data is very difficult to compile because employment is largely seasonal and casual, spread over a large number of workplaces. In addition, some of the catering workers are entered as 'hospital workers', or 'local authority workers' in official statistics. However, the figure of two million is frequently presented as a reasonable estimate of all those working in the hotel and catering sector. The *Statistical Review of the Hotel and Catering Industry*, published by the Catering Intelligence Unit in association with the industry's Training Board, gives a figure of 1,680,000 for 1982, which excludes those working in local authority, educational, NHS and welfare catering. The Department of the Employment gives a figure of 1,069,000 (of whom 689,000 are women and of these 504,000 work part-time) for hotel and catering in June 1986 which excludes all the above as well as in-house company catering. The two sets of figures are estimated on the basis of different models, but they are consistent with the overall figure of two million. The numbers of those in commercial catering has risen from 698,000 in 1970, to 826,000 in 1975, to 1,013,000 in 1980, to the present 1,069,000. See *Employment Gazette*, October 1986, and *Annual Abstract of Statistics*, 1985.

2 At the time of the field research (1984), waitresses earned a gross average of £76.30 per week excluding overtime, female kitchen hands £79.40, hairdressers £66.80, shop assistants £79.50, machinists £77.70 and cleaners £86.20. The average for all manual full-time women employees was £90.80. Among men, bar staff earned £108.50, cooks £117.00 and hospital porters £111.20. Farm workers earned £105.00, while the average for all manual workers was £148.80 (*New Earnings Survey*, 1984. All figures include earnings of employees whose earnings were affected by absence). Part-time earnings of catering workers are the lowest of all. In 1984, they earned an hourly average of £1.87 and a weekly average of £32.20, against national averages for all industries and services of £2.10 per hour and £39.70 per week.

3 British statistics on the size of the service industries in *Social Trends*, 1984 and 1985 and *Economic Trends*, 1984 and 1985. For estimates of the size of the service sector in the United States, see Rothschild, 1981, and Heskett, 1986. For European statistics on the shift from manufacturing to the tertiary sector, see Gershuny and Miles, 1983.
4 For the classic optimistic statement of the 'goods to services thesis', see Bell, 1974; for a more recent optimistic assessment of the prospects of the service sector, see Heskett, 1986.
5 'Women's employment in 1984 was concentrated in the industries which had expanded since 1971, that is, the service industries apart from transport and communication,' *Social Trends*, 1985:65. It is not accidental that the shift of employment to the service sector coincides with two other long-term trends in employment – the increasing proportion of part-time workers and the increasing numbers of women in the workforce. Part-time employment has doubled in the last 20 years and now accounts for about 21 per cent of those in employment as against 15 per cent in 1971. About nine out of ten part-time workers are female. The composition of the civilian labourforce in Great Britain in the past 25 years has changed as follows:

Year	Men	Women	Married Women
1961	16.1	7.7	3.9
1971	15.6	9.3	5.8
1981	15.6	10.6	6.7
1986	(15.6)	(11.5)	–

All figures in millions. Reproduced from *Social Trends*.

For similar trends in the United States and a convincing illustration of the low quality of service jobs, see Rothschild, 1981.
6 Reproduced from *Time* magazine, 30 May 1983.
7 Even a brief outline of the different positions is beyond the scope of this book. Some of the many interesting contributions, see Handy, 1984; Gershuny and Miles, 1983; Heskett, 1986; Stonier, 1982; and Merritt, 1982.
8 See, for instance, Gersuny and Rosengren, 1973; Lewis, 1973; Channon, 1978; Cowell, 1984; and Heskett, 1986.
9 As a 'people's industry', catering seemed an ideal ground in the 1940s for testing the ideas of the Human Relations school of management as well as for putting these ideas into practice; the advocates of this school argued that organizational success is dependent on management's ability to motivate individuals by promoting informal group bonds and enhancing their employees' sense of pride and individuality in their work. Management's task in achieving good human relations, it was argued, goes beyond a pat on the back and an annual get-together and must proceed from a recognition that workers are human – that they do not simply act out their parts as automata. Workers are distinct individuals, with personal likes and

dislikes, prides and prejudices, strengths and weaknesses; as members of social groups, workers also share in the values, norms and standards of the groups to which they belong.

10 'Discretion is the enemy of order, standardization and quality,' Levitt, 1972:44.

11 Of course, Levitt and his colleagues at the Harvard Business School are not the first to indicate the significance of technological arrangements for the service industry. W. F. Whyte had discussed the difference that the innocent 'spindle' (a spike on which orders are attached in sequence) can make in improving communication and reducing tension between cooks and waiters. What, however, sharply distinguishes the two approaches is Levitt's systematic attempt to replace the human factor with methodical planning and careful application of technological software and hardware. Levitt regards technology as an assortment of machines, products, recipes and 'ways of doing things', carefully deployed according to a plan aimed at optimizing output. The smallest as well as the largest things *are* technology in as much as they are part of a carefully designed mechanism; a specially designed bag for fried potatoes is 'technology', just as McDonald's as a whole 'is an example of a soft technology' (1972:48). Using this broad definition of technology, Levitt scorns to distinguish it from the 'principles of Scientific Management'. I am in general agreement with this broad conceptualization of technology.

12 In a frequently criticized but pioneering study, Blauner argued that mass production is responsible for the experience of alienation at work. By contrast, fully automated process production is seen as restoring for the worker the meaning of work and a sense of control over the work process. Blauner's theory is based on data drawn from four manufacturing industries, and although it has provoked a considerable controversy it has not to my knowledge been tested in the service sector. See Blauner, 1964.

13 For some of the major contributions to the debate sparked off by Braverman's book, see Hill, 1981; Littler and Salaman, 1982; Burawoy, 1981 and 1985; Friedman, 1977; Wood, 1982; Zimbalist, 1979; Gershuny, 1978; and Edwards, 1979. Even a small summary of the contributions to this debate is beyond the scope of this book. Several of the points raised by various contributors, however, will be discussed in the course of the analysis of the research findings.

14 For an extremely informative recent account of the world of the waiters in quality establishments based on participant observation, see Mars and Nicod, 1984. While research into catering is limited it is not nonexistent. In his pioneering piece of research carried out in hotels and restaurants in Chicago in the 1940s, William Foote Whyte argued that the friction between waitresses and cooks (or pantry-staff) is not merely a case of conflict of roles, but the results of different values attached by the first group to quick service in the right order of delivery, and by the latter group to the quality of the meal and the presentation. The fact that most serving staff were female and most cooking staff

Notes to page 12

male made the conflict more acute: male cooks could not stand being given orders and shouted at by female waitresses. For Whyte, the waitresses shouting and complaining had become a trademark of their profession because it was a psychological device of 'letting off steam' in one social transaction, while preserving a cheerful and polite front in their transactions with the clients. Whyte insisted that it was the management's task to reduce such work pressures:

> How then can management take the pressure off? That is a problem of supervision, and it has many aspects that we cannot take up here; but it should be emphasized that skillful supervision begins with giving employees an opportunity to talk their problems off their chests. If the worker cannot be allowed to express his emotions to the customer, then some other outlet must be provided, for bottled up emotions inevitably take up their toll on the nervous system and reflect in poor work performance. (Whyte, 1946:147)

Whyte, in spite of his human relations orientation, showed a remarkable appreciation of some aspects of catering technology, such as the 'spindle', on the workers' experiences at work. Unfortunately nobody seems to have picked up this line of inquiry. Neither Boas Shamir in his study of workplace relations in eight English hotels, nor Angela Bowey in her five case studies of restaurants deal in any length with the implications of technology for work-relations or with the nature of control (Shamir, 1975; Bowey, 1976). Instead, they both concentrate on organizational factors, such as the degree of formality, the number of levels in the hierarchy and so on. The importance of these factors is beyond doubt, but they must be seen as intimately linked with technological requirements as well as requirements of control (Braverman, 1974; Woodward, 1965). Both Shamir's and Bowey's studies provide a wealth of insights concerning the pressures and tensions present in hotels and restaurants, the function of tipping and the orientations of service workers, without, however, clarifying the issues of skill, control and technology.

An excellent and at times entertaining account of trouble-spots in a hotel chain is given by Doswell and Nailon in *Case Studies in Hotel Management*, but their purposes are illustrative rather than analytical (Doswell and Nailon, 1967). Equally valuable is Chivers' study based on responses from 629 hotel and hospital chefs and cooks, offering a sensitive account of the historical developments of their trade (Chivers, 1972). He also gives a detailed description of the pros and cons of their jobs, recalling Orwell's classic descriptions of waiters and plongeurs in *Down and Out In Paris and London* (Orwell, 1933). Chivers tries to distinguish whether cooks form part of the working class or whether they have realistic chances of moving into the middle class, but the criteria which he uses seem questionable; he believes that if a cook aspires to a career in catering he/she firmly belongs to the working class, while only if he/she aspires to a business of his own is he/she a member of the middle class. It is also regrettable that he relates only a few details of his survey findings and methodology.

More recently, Wood and Pedler, and Macfarlane, have given excellent accounts of industrial relations based on case studies in catering establishments (Wood and Pedler, 1978; Macfarlane, 1982). In their articles, they discuss the special problems encountered by trade unions trying to organize in catering, and managerial attitudes towards unions and collective bargaining. Their studies highlight that in vast numbers of catering establishments low wages for casual or part-time workers are still regarded as a key condition for economic viability by management and that, although catering may be trying to move into the high-tech management approach of manufacturing, wages and conditions of work for catering staff are still those associated with labour-intensive, petty entrepreneurial concerns; the glamour image created for modern catering establishments by marketing experts may conceal sordid working realities.

From a purely theoretical point of view, one of the most interesting studies in the catering industry is Beynon's and Blackburn's – unfortunately, however, this study, based on a factory manufacturing luxury foods, did not address the service component of catering and the proliferation of soft technologies in this sector (Beynon and Blackburn, 1972). Their account draws attention to the complex nature of the workers' attitudes towards their work which precludes a straightforward technological determination; both workplace and social and personal factors influence people's attitudes towards their work. At the same time, their account suggests what is explicit in Beynon's subsequent and better-known work, *Working for Ford* – that technology represents a constant 'frontier of control', an object of bargaining and negotiation in the antagonistic relationship between management and workers (Beynon, 1973).

The plausibility of this proposition has not, to my knowledge, been tested in the service industry; nor has the plausibility of the propositions relating technology with levels of skill and alienation been examined in any detail in this industry. What does seem to be beyond doubt, however, is that catering is unlikely to preserve its traditional image for very much longer. In the report *Innovation and Change in the Hotel and Catering Industry* (1983), published by that industry's Training Board, it is suggested that different sectors of catering are responding to the current economic recession with a substantial wave of technological innovation and a re-appraisal of management thinking on efficiency and productivity. One of the interesting aspects of the study is that its concept of technology is a broad one, including both hardware and software, i.e. not only new machines and equipment for cooking, serving and administration but also 'new ways of doing things'. What needs to be investigated is the effectiveness of such changes, their implications for people working in the industry, and the opposition which management may encounter in implementing them.

15 Apart from haute-cuisine restaurants, the most conspicuous absences from my sample are hotel and industrial catering. Hotel catering is complicated by the relations between the catering and other

departments within each hotel and, like restaurants, it would have been difficult to find a few representative ones. For extensive and insightful discussions of this section of catering, see Mars, 1982; and Mars and Nicod, 1984. Much of industrial catering operates on a similar basis as the first two mass catering establishments in this study.

16 In addition to the experiences of the workers in these eight establishments the book draws on the catering experiences of some of my students. Having been involved in the teaching of industrial sociology and related subjects to first-year undergraduates over a number of years, I found that many of them (about one in ten, in some classes) had some experience of working in catering. I decided to ask for the help of those of my students who had worked in catering and over a period of eighteen months I interviewed some twenty-five of them. In addition, many of them provided me with extremely useful information on the training and work methods of some of the large fast-food chains.

Although I used the same interview schedule, my students' responses are not really equivalent to those of my original respondents. In the first place, they all come from a highly specific population, that of students obtaining casual work in catering. Second, they already knew me and their responses were influenced by my relation to them as teacher to student. Third, they were already familiar with the field of academic research within which this project took place. Most importantly, however, unlike my field respondents, they were interviewed away from the workplace and in some cases a considerable time after the termination of their employment. Their responses, however, have illustrated and amplified some of the points made by the other respondents, and some of them had worked in establishments in which it would have been impossible to obtain permission to carry out research. For these reasons, although their responses have not been included in the statistical data, many of their comments and views are reproduced in the pages of this book.

Chapter 1 Home-cooking for thousands

1 See Steele and Delaney (1983).
2 Cf. Mars who argues that by recruiting people without catering experience management tries to crack down on pilfering and fiddles at work (Mars, 1982:193).
3 See Johan Galtung (1967) and Paul Lazarsfeld (1958).
4 The content of this table must be accepted with caution; 'I don't have time to get bored,' I was told time and again by workers on my survey. Some of those who said their jobs were interesting admitted that they would prefer something more challenging.
5 Burawoy has looked in detail into the competition among workers over the distribution of good and bad jobs; this arises not only in

capitalist factories but also state run factories in countries like Hungary. See Burawoy, 1985:173.
6 All national figures, from the *New Earnings Survey*, 1985.
7 See, for example, Pond, 1983.
8 It is remarkable that all dining-room assistants who belonged to the union, except for the three supervisors, described themselves as committed unionists. The only three cooks who described themselves in these terms were also women. Unlike the workers in a tobacco plant studied by Anna Pollert (1981:159ff), these women were not ignorant about unions, did not regard unions as part of a 'man's world' and did not feel that their femininity excluded them from unions.
9 Mars makes a similar point based on his research in hotels. He argues that there is a *core* of workers who collude with management and reap a large number of informal rewards and a *periphery* who have to contend with doing everything 'by the book'. Miss Campbell's reference to a 'syndicate' gives precisely this picture. See Mars, 1982:194.

Chapter 2 The cooking factory

1 Although dining-assistants had greater job autonomy than cook-freeze workers their Job Index scores were lower (average 13.1 against 14.3). This is accounted by the larger numbers of cook-freeze workers who saw promotion as a realistic prospect, who said that their job required concentration and who found that there were short-cuts in their job.
2 Such comments cast serious doubts on the relevance of the council's very strict regulations concerning the nutritional content of schoolmeals (e.g. 81 gm of vegetable per child, salad of at least five items including a fruit item at least once per week, etc.). While the earlier free meals led to great waste as children did not finish their food, the cafeteria system meant that many children could not afford or simply chose not to have the nutritious items on the menu.
3 For a very similar picture, see Gamarnikow et al., 1983; one of the school-meals women interviewed by Sheila Cunnison said 'Let's face it, we're all here because of what there is at the end of the week.' Cunnison discusses the function of the women's earnings as part of the family budget and provides an interesting discussion of the women's radicalization during the 1979 'winter of discontent'.
4 *Employment Gazette*, September 1984, and *New Earnings Survey*, 1983.
5 The dignity of work is an important issue for catering workers internationally. It was one of the workers' main grievances during the hotel workers strike in San Francisco in the summer of 1980. The employers, in the press briefings, complained that 'economic issues were mixed with calls for the employers to treat the employees "with dignity" and other such emotional requirements. ... The Union has

said that the non-economic demands are more important than the economic ones.' For an informative discussion, see Richmond, 1981.

Chapter 3 The fun food machine

1 Quoted in Braverman, 1974:371.
2 See *Catering Times*, October 1983.
3 As Henry Ford put it: 'We regulated the speed of men by the speed of the conveyor' (1931:39).
4 Figures from the *New Earnings Survey*, 1983.
5 See Macfarlane, 1982:36.
6 Nichols and Beynon (1977) have made this point most forcefully: 'During this century the working classes of Europe and America have been systematically *deskilled* by the "progress" of capitalist production. And with this deskilling has come a contempt for work' (pp. 17–18). See also p. 193.
7 What few fast-food managers will tell you is that *it pays* to employ young workers, whose living expenses are subsidized by their parents. This is especially true for 17-year-olds who only get paid 70 per cent of the adult wage as set down by the Wages' Councils. It is not accidental that about one in three of fast food workers are 16 or 17.
8 Gorz captures the casual and temporary attitude of fast-food workers in his description of a new non-class of non-workers who

> do not feel they belong to the working class, *or to any other class*. They do not recognize themselves in the term 'worker' or in its symmetrical opposite, 'unemployed'. Whether they work in a bank, the civil service, a cleaning agency or a factory, neo-proletarians are basically non-workers temporarily doing something that means nothing to them. They do 'any old thing' which 'anyone' could do, provisionally engaged in temporary and nameless work. (1982:68)

However, my respondents' favourable attitudes towards unions and their hopes of obtaining 'proper jobs' and 'settling down' to a more permanent and stable existence suggest that their stint in fast food may be more a traineeship into the working class than permanent membership of a non-class.

Chapter 4 Craft cooking for gentlemen

1 In order to protect the confidentiality of my interviewees in a small establishment like Saint George's a few small details have been altered.
2 See, for example, Wood, 1982:17:

> A consideration of workers' resistance opens up the issue of the social construction of skill – that is, the question of whether certain

workers or jobs are labelled skilled even though the content of their work is largely unskilled. Two extreme versions of the argument that skill is socially constructed are possible. First, one might stress the way in which the labels attached to certain jobs are created or maintained by managements as a way of coping with worker resistance, as they are used to segment and reduce the power and cohesion of the working class. Alternatively, labels might be seen as the direct result of workers' resistance or initiatives: strongly organized groups of workers might secure for themselves a level of wages normally or previously associated with apprenticeship-trained workers and may even create and control their own apprenticeship system, designed to reinforce exclusive unionism rather than to provide a necessary and comprehensive training.

3 For a discussion of tacit skills, see Manwaring and Wood, 1984.
4 This is not to say that all workers would be happy in the cosy, personal atmosphere of Saint George's. The sixth member of staff said: 'I've liked it here and when you are older you don't like to chop and change. But I was happier in the factory job. I liked working with a lot of people.' This confirms Ingham's view that some people's expectations may be better met by a more impersonal and bureaucratic organization. The attitudes and experiences of the staff at Saint George's Club, however, do not confirm the same author's view that small firm workers are a self-selected group with a more intrinsic orientation to work than workers of large firms. All six women had earlier worked in large-scale catering operations and it was circumstance rather than choice that took them to Saint George's. Moreover, 'interest and variety' did *not* figure prominently in these women's work orientations. See Ingham, 1967 and 1970. The very small size of the sample at Saint George's permits no generalizations as to the work attitudes of 'all' small firm workers – for extensive and insightful discussions of this sector of the workforce, see Curran and Stanworth 1979, 1981a and 1982.

Chapter 5 The small independent restaurant or café

1 See Mintel, 1983.
2 There is some variation depending on the statistical source one relies on. *Social Trends* (1985:65) gives the figure of 2,433,000 for the number of self-employed in June 1984, while the *Employment Gazette* (November 1984:477) quotes the figure of a report by the Manpower Services Commission as 2.25 million for March 1984.
3 *Social Trends*, 1985.
4 *Employment Gazette*, 1984, Table 11.4.
5 Control in these small catering establishments is personal, direct and *ad hoc*. This is what Richard Edwards (1979) has described as 'simple' control in contrast to the technical and bureaucratic controls. It is similar to what Joan Woodward (1970) identified as 'personal' control.

Workplace politics and the relations between employers and employees in small firms are strongly influenced by this type of control. The fact that small firms tend to be friendlier places to work was central to the findings of the pioneering Bolton Report on small firms (1971); however, the report's conclusion that small firms are relatively conflict-free has been questioned by subsequent research on small firms. See Newby, 1975; Curran and Stanworth, 1981b and 1982; and Scott and Rainnie, 1982.

6 Since the publication of the Bolton Report (1971), an increasing amount of information on the working conditions, work attitudes and job satisfaction of self-employed individuals and owners of small firms has started to surface. The Bolton Report presented a portrait of small businessmen based on their own self-descriptions – they were seen as resilient individuals, for whom economic independence rather than rapid financial gain was the main goal. Many of them felt besieged by banks, competitors, local and central government, and misunderstood by the wider public. This portrait, which fits remarkably well the owners of the two restaurants described in this chapter, has since been refined, but its central features have been generally confirmed. See Curran and Stanworth, 1982:12ff, for an informative overview. The longtitudinal survey being conducted by the National Child Development Study provides much useful data on the self-employed. A cohort of 12,538 individuals born in March 1958 is being regularly interviewed. In 1981, at the age of 23, 4.7 per cent of the respondents were self-employed, three-quarters of whom did not employ other workers. Nearly 40 per cent of the self-employed males worked for 50 hours per week or more (in contrast to only 17 per cent of the waged workers) and 80 per cent worked unsociable hours. However, a higher proportion of the self-employed expressed satisfaction with various aspects of their work. Thirty-eight per cent of the self-employed men without employees, 44 per cent of those with employees and 53 per cent of the self-employed women said they were 'very satisfied' with their job as a whole; only 24 per cent of male wage-earners and 32 per cent of female expressed similar satisfaction. Self-employed women and self-employed men without employees were more likely to be very satisfied if they worked in a family business. See Joan Payne (1984).

Conclusions: Keeping the lid on

1 For a discussion of the 'twilight trades', see Pearson, 1985.
2 See *New Earnings Survey*, 1983.
3 This index was based on respondents' answers to nine questions concerning the autonomy they experienced in their work (short-cuts, personal touches, improvisation, etc.) as well as some more general features of their job (promotion, tiredness, etc.) The index was additive and answers were coded on a three-point scale. The higher an individual's score on the index the higher the objective quality of

Notes to page 163

his/her job. Like other indices of this type it suffered from an *ad hoc* quality; moreover, due to the relatively small size of the sample it was not possible to weigh the different items on the index through factor analysis. Finally, although the index tried to capture the job's objective quality, it was compiled on the basis of subjective evaluations.

Although there were individual variations in the Job Index scores, the scores of people doing the same work were substantially similar; for example 19 out of 26 fast-food workers scored between 12 and 16; 15 of the 19 cooks at Saint Theresa's scored between 17 and 21, while all the trolley-porters scored between 11 and 15; 13 out of 17 cook-freeze staff scored between 12 and 16. Some of the individual variations are due to different perceptions and some to genuine differences in the work done even by workers with the same job description.

4 Two groups, however, deviate from this trend. Kitchen-porters who, in spite of their low satisfaction, scored high on the Job Index and the staff in the minor dining areas at Michael Lansby, who were quite satisfied in spite of the low scores on the Job Index. This is true to a lesser extent of staff in the other dining areas. Various reasons can account for these variations. The kitchen-porters scored high on the Job Index because of the craft environment in which they worked; many of them did exactly the same tasks as cooks (although some were perpetually buried by mountains of washing-up). Much of their dissatisfaction was the result of feeling unfairly treated as perpetual underdogs. The serving staff in the minor areas at Michael Lansby, and to a lesser extent workers in other dining-areas, were satisfied in jobs with low scores on the index. In reality, however, their jobs were not at all unfulfilling. The relative absence of supervision, the informal relations they developed with the clients and the small size of their work units made their jobs interesting and rewarding.

183

Bibliography and further reading

Bell, D. (1974), *The Coming of Post-Industrial Society*, Heinemann.
Beynon H. (1973), *Working for Ford*, Penguin.
Beynon H. and Blackburn R. M. (1972), *Perceptions of Work*, Cambridge University Press.
Blackwell T. and Seabrook J. (1985), *A World Still to Win – The Reconstruction of the Post-War Working Class*, Faber & Faber.
Blauner R. (1964), *Alienation and Freedom*, Chicago University Press.
Bowey A. M. (1976), *The Sociology of Organizations*, Hodder & Stoughton.
Braverman H. (1974), *Labor and Monopoly Capital*, Monthly Review Press.
Burawoy M. (1981), 'Terrains of Contest: Factory and State Under Capitalism and Socialism', *Socialist Review*, vol. 11, no. 4.
Burawoy M. (1985), *The Politics of Production*, Verso.
Channon D. F. (1978), *The Service Industries*, Macmillan.
Chivers T. S. (1972), 'The Proletarianization of a Service Worker', *Sociological Review*, pp. 633–56.
Cohen P. (1985), 'Towards Youthtopia?' *Marxism Today*, October.
Cowell D. W. (1984), *The Marketing of Services*, Heinemann.
Curran J. and Stanworth J. (1979), 'Worker Involvement and Social Relations in the Small Firm', *Sociological Review*, Vol. 27, No. 2.
Curran J. and Stanworth J. (1981a), 'A New Look at Job Satisfaction in the Small Firm', *Human Relations*, vol. 34, no. 5.
Curran J. and Stanworth J. (1981b), 'The Social Dynamics of Small Manufacturing Enterprise', *Journal of Management Studies*, vol. 18, no. 2. Curran J. and Stanworth J. (1982), 'Bolton Ten Years On – A Research Inventory and Critical Review' in J. Stanworth et al. (eds), *Perspectives on a Decade of Small Business Research – Bolton Ten Years On*, Gower.
Doswell R. and Nailon P. (1967), *Case Studies in Hotel Management*, Barrie & Jenkins.
Edwards R. (1979), *Contested Terrain: The Transformation of the Workplace in the Twentieth Century*, Basic Books.
Evans J. (1974), *Catering in Schools and Colleges*, Barrie & Jenkins.
Ford H. (1923), *My Life and My Work*, Heinemann.
Ford H. (1931), *Moving Forward*, Heinemann.

Friedman A. (1977), 'Responsible Autonomy Versus Direct Control over the Labour Process', *Capital and Class*, no. 1.
Fuchs V. (1968), *The Service Economy*, National Bureau of Economic Research, New York.
Galtung J. (1967), *Theory and Methods of Social Research*, Allen & Unwin.
Gamarnikow E. et al. (eds) (1983), *Gender, Class and Work*, Heinemann.
Gershuny J. I. (1978), *After Industrial Society*, Macmillan.
Gershuny J. I. and I. D. Miles (1983), *The New Service Economy*, Frances Pinter.
Gersuny C. and W. R. Rosengren (1973), *The Service Society*, Schenkman.
Giddens A. (1973), *The Class Structure of the Advanced Societies*, Harper & Row.
Ginsberg E. (1982), 'The Mechanization of Work', *Scientific American*, vol. 247, no. 3.
Giuliano V. E. (1982), 'The Mechanization of Office Work', *Scientific American*, vol. 247, no. 3.
Goldthorpe J. H. et al. (1968), *The Affluent Worker*, Cambridge University Press.
Gorz A. (1982), *Farewell to the Working Class*, Pluto Press.
Handy C. (1984), *The Future of Work*, Blackwell.
Heskett J. L. (1986), *Managing in the Service Economy*, Harvard Business School.
Hill S. (1981), *Competition and Control at Work*, Heinemann.
Ingham G. (1967), 'Organizational Size, Orientation to Work and Industrial Behaviour', *Sociology*, vol. 1, pp. 239–58.
Ingham G. (1970), *Size of Industrial Organisation and Worker Behaviour*, Cambridge University Press.
Innovation and Change in the Hotel and Catering Industry (1983), Hotel and Catering Industry Training Board.
Lazarsfeld P. F. (1958), 'Evidence and Inference in Social Research', *Daedalus*, no. 87, pp. 99–130.
Levitt T. (1972), 'Production-Line Approach to Service', *Harvard Business Review*, September–October.
Levitt T. (1981), 'Marketing Intangible Products and Product Intangibles', *The Cornell HRA Quarterly*, August.
Lewis R. (1973), *The New Service Society*, Longman.
Littler C. R. and Salaman G. (1982), 'Bravermania and Beyond – Recent Theories of the Labour Process', *Sociology*, vol. 16, no. 2.
Macfarlane A. (1982), 'Trade Union Growth, the Employer and the Hotel and Restaurant Industry: A Case Study', *Industrial Relations Journal*, Winter, pp. 29–43.
McGary V. E. and Donaldson B. (1969), 'A Model of Centralized Tray Assembly Conveyor System for a Hospital', *Journal of American Dietetic Association*, October.
Manwaring T. and Wood S. (1984), 'The Ghost in the Machine: Tacit Skills and the Labor Process', *Socialist Review*, vol. 14, no. 2.
Mars G. (1982), *Cheats at Work*, Allen & Unwin.
Mars G. and M. Nicod (1984), *The World of Waiters*, Allen & Unwin.
Merritt G. (1982), *World Out of Work*, Collins.

Bibliography and further reading

Newby H. (1975), 'The Deferential Dialectic', *Comparative Studies in Society and History*, vol. 17, no. 2.
Nichols T. and Beynon H. (1977), *Living with Capitalism: Class Relations and the Modern Factory*, Routledge & Kegan Paul.
Orwell G. (1933), *Down and Out in Paris and London*, Penguin, 1966.
Payne J. (1984), 'Young Self-Employed Workers', *Employment Gazette*, November.
Pearson P. (1985), *Twilight Robbery: Low Paid Workers in Britain Today*, Pluto Press.
Pollert A. (1981), *Girls, Wives, Factory Lives*, Macmillan.
Pond C. (1983), 'Wages Councils, the Unorganised, and the Low Paid', in Bain G. S. (ed.), *Industrial Relations in Britain*, Blackwell.
Purcell J. (1982), 'Macho Managers and the New Industrial Relations', *Employee Relations*, vol. 4, no. 1.
Richmond A. (1981), 'The San Francisco Hotel Strike', *Socialist Review*, vol. 11, no. 3.
Robins D. and Cohen P. (1978), *Knuckle Sandwich*, Penguin.
Robins D. (1984), *We Hate Humans*, Penguin.
Rothschild E. (1981), 'Reagan and the Real America', *The New York Review of Books*, 5 February.
Scott M. and A. Rainnie (1982), 'Beyond Bolton – Industrial Relations in the Small Firm', in ed. J. Stanworth et al, *Perspectives on a Decade of Small Business Research – Bolton Ten Years On*, Gower.
Shamir B. (1975), 'Between Bureaucracy and Hospitality – Some Organizational Characteristics of Hotels'. *Journal of Management Studies*, Vol. 15, No. 3, 1978.
Small Firms – Report of the Committee of Inquiry on Small Firms (The Bolton Report) (1971), Cmnd. 4811, HMSO.
Stanworth J., A. Westrip, D. Watkins and J. Lewis (1982), *Perspectives on a Decade of Small Business Research – Bolton Ten Years On*, Gower.
Statistical Review of the Hotel and Catering Industry (1984), Catering Intelligence Unit.
Steele G. S. G. and D. Delaney (1983), *Scrutiny Programme: The Cost of Catering in the NHS*, DHSS.
Stonier T. (1982), *The Wealth of Information: A Profile of the Post-Industrial Society*, Methuen.
Taylor F. W. (1967), *The Principles of Scientific Management*, Harper & Row.
Thompson P. and Bannon E. (1985), *Working the System: The Shop Floor and New*, Pluto Press.
Thorpe D., *The Catering Industry*, Research Report 29, Retail Outlets Research Unit, Manchester Business School, Report no. 29, November 1977.
Whyte W. F. (1948), *Human Relations in the Restaurant Industry*, McGraw-Hill.
Whyte W. F. (1946), 'When Workers and Customers Meet', in Whyte (ed.), *Industry and Society*, McGraw-Hill.
Whyte W. F. (1949), 'The Social Structure of the Restaurant', *American Journal of Sociology*, vol. 54, pp. 302–10.
Willis P. (1978), *Learning to Labour*, Saxon House.

Wood S. and Pedler M. (1978), 'On Losing their Virginity – The Story of a Strike at the Grosvenor Hotel, Sheffield', *Industrial Relations Journal*, vol. 9, no. 2.
Wood S. (ed.) (1982), *The Degradation of Work?*, Hutchinson.
Woodward J. (1965), *Industrial Organization*, Oxford University Press.
Woodward J. (ed.) (1970), *Industrial Organization: Behaviour and Control*, Oxford University Press.
Wright E. O. (1985), *Classes*, Verso.
Zimbalist A. (1979), *Case Studies on the Labor Process*, Monthly Review Press.

Statistical sources

Annual Abstract of Statistics, 1985.
Economic Trends, 1984 and 1985.
Employment Gazette, 1984 and 1985.
Mintel, *Market Intelligence*, November 1982 and August 1983.
New Earnings Survey, 1983, 1984 and 1985.
Social Trends, 1984 and 1985.

Index

absenteeism, 53, 168
alienation, 87ff, 163
altruistic orientation towards work, 27, 73f
ambivalence and volatility of attitudes, 15, 28, 113, 122ff
arrogance, allegations of management, 43, 46, 79, 82ff, 117

Bell, D., 5, 174
Beynon, H., 26, 85, 92, 107, 177, 180
Blackburn R. M., 177
Blackwell, T., 156
Blauner, R., 88, 89, 175
Bolton Report, 182
Bowey, A. M., 176
Braverman, H., 9ff, 88, 138, 175, 176, 180
Burawoy, M., 79, 107, 166, 175, 178, 179

catering: the industry, 2, 7ff, 153ff, 173; in the National Health Service, Ch. 1, 160; as part of the service sector, 4ff; technology, 7ff, 11ff, 57ff, 87ff, 95, 125ff, 162ff; *see also* technology
catering workers: low pay, 173, *see also* earnings; low status of, 3, 85ff, 158, 179
Channon, D. F., 174

Chivers, T. S., 129, 176
choices, feeling of having, 27, 34ff, 121, 158
clerical workers, 27
closed-shop, 84ff
Cohen, P., 109, 122
Cowell, D. W., 174
control, 7, 177; types of management, 52, 81, 115, 146; resistance to management, 107, 163; workers' sphere of, 31f, 71, 82, 89, 166ff
cultural backgrounds of catering workers, 2, 15, 153
Cunnison, S., 179
Curran, J., 181, 182

Delaney D., 178
deskilling, 9ff, 88ff, 180, *see also* skill, control, Taylor F. W.
dignity of work, *see* catering workers, low status of
discontents of catering workers, 34, 40ff, 44ff, 53ff, 66ff, 76ff, 90ff, 101ff, 166ff
discrimination, experience of, 38, 45ff
Doswell R., 176

earnings of catering workers, 3, 39ff, 75ff, 108ff, 135ff, 159ff, 179
economic recession, its effects on workers' attitudes, 40ff, 154ff

Index

Edwards, R., 52, 81, 115, 146, 166, 175, 181

family obligations, women workers', 61f, 91, 132, 135
fantasies and dreams, workers', 92, 105, 112, 121, 149, 161
fast food, 8, 59, Chapter 3, 163, 167; reliance on young workers, 97, 126ff, 180
fiddles and pilfering in catering, 29ff, 37, 52
Ford H., 10, 125, 180
fragmentation, task, 59, 79, *see also* Taylor F. W., skill and deskilling
Friedman, A., 175
Fuchs, V., 6

Galtung, J., 178
Gamarnikow, E., 179
games and shortcuts as ways of asserting control, 34ff, 106, 108, 163
Gershuny, J. I., 5, 6, 174, 175
Gersuny C., 174
Giddens, A., 150
Golthorpe, J. H., 24ff
Gorz, A., 81, 126, 180
group bonds among workers, 48, 51, 89ff, 110ff, 133ff

Handy, C., 174
'having a laugh', as survival mechanism, 90, 161
Heskett, J. L., 174
Hill, S., 175
Human Relations school, 174ff

Iacocca, L., 5
industrial relations, *see* unions, workplace politics
Ingham, G., 139, 181
instrumental orientation to work, 25ff, 63ff, 156ff, *see also* job, expectations and orientations towards
intrinsic orientation to work, 27, 33, 62, 99ff, 160, *see also* job,

expectations and orientations towards

job: autonomy in the, 30ff, 68, 71, 74, 89, 106ff, 161ff; expectations and orientations towards, 24ff, 62ff, 74, 99ff, 133ff, 156ff, 160; 'gravy jobs' and 'stinkers', 36, 38, 166; satisfaction and dissatisfaction, 28ff, 38, 54, 66ff, 99ff, 104, 134ff, 160ff; security, 24, 99; as a trap, 26, 55, 69, 120, 157

Lazarsfeld, P., 178
Levitt, T., 7ff, 11, 125, 175
Lewis, R., 174
Littler, C. R., 175

management, 41ff, 77ff; control, 52ff, 166ff; divisive tactics, 51ff; favouritism and arbitrariness as method of control, 36, 52; 'macho', 42, 165; power of, 52ff, 81ff, 114ff; 'styles', 41, 78ff; workers' attitudes towards, 43ff, 76ff, 116ff
managers: job satisfaction and dissatisfaction, 54, 80, 84, 86, 111ff, 161; how they spend their time, 77, 113ff
Macfarlane, A., 177, 180
Manwaring, T., 139, 181
Mars, G., 175, 178, 179
Merritt, G., 174
Miles, I. D., 5, 174
monotony and boredom, 35, 39, 66ff, 74, 76, 101ff, 105, 107

Nailon, P., 176
Nichols, T., 26, 85, 180
Nicod, M., 175, 178

Orwell, G., 138, 176
overtime, 45, 54

part-time workers, 87, 97, 174
pay, *see* earnings
Payne, J., 182

189

Index

Pearson, P., 182
Pedler, M., 177
political environment, its effects on workers' attitudes, 154ff, 157ff, 166
Pollert, A., 85, 87, 179
Pond, C., 179
powerlessness and attempts to establish control, 26, 82, 89ff, 106ff, 118, 160, 162ff, 165ff, *see also* control, workplace politics
promotion, attitudes towards, 27, 99, 122, 124
Purcell, J., 42, 165

Rainnie, A., 182
'realism', workers' new, 40ff, 78, 155, 165ff
recruitment, 21, 127ff
Richmond, A., 180
Robins, D., 109, 122
Rosengren, W. R., 174
Rothschild, E., 88, 174
rules and regulations, 42, 106ff, 115, 167

Salaman, G., 175
Scott, M., 182
Seabrook, J., 156
self-employment in catering, Chapter 5, 160ff, 182
service industries, 4ff, 156, 174
schoolmeals catering, 72ff
Shamir, B., 176
shiftwork and rosters, 20, 41ff
skill, 11, 32, 36, 68, 105, 125ff, 137ff, 161ff, 181, *see also* deskilling, training, control and technology
small organizations, working in, 139ff, Chapter 5, 167, 181
Stanworth, J., 181, 182
Steele, G. S. G., 178
Stonier, T., 174
survival mechanisms, 161ff;

comradeship, 90ff, 110ff;
'creating own space', 37, 89;
temporary orientation, 120ff, *see also* fantasies, games, fiddles, and 'having a laugh'

Taylor, F. W. and Taylorism, 10, 59, 80, 107, 175
technology, 7ff, 57ff, 68ff, 71ff, 79ff, 87ff, 95ff, 124ff, 161ff, 167ff, 175, 177
training and lack of, 30, 58, 104, 132

unemployment: experience of, 120ff; fear of, 55, 156ff;
unions, 154ff; in catering, 48ff; workers' attitudes towards, 49ff, 84ff, 119ff

Whyte, W. F., 175, 176
Willis, P., 90, 126
women workers, Chapter 2, 137ff; in catering, 46, 87, 179; in the service sector, 5
'women's jobs', 76, 137, 139
Wood, S., 139, 175, 177, 180, 181
Woodward J., 176, 181
workgroups and teamwork, 51, 90ff, 110ff, 133
workplace politics, 164ff; at Saint Theresa's, 20ff; at Michael Lansby, 77ff; in smaller organizations, 146, 181
Wright, E. O., 149

young workers, 94, 97, 158ff, 180; temporary orientation towards their job, 97, 120, 122ff; wages, 109ff

Zimbalist, A., 175